THE NEXT AMERICAN ECONOMY

THE
NEXT AMERICAN
ECONOMY

Blueprint for a Real Recovery

WILLIAM J. HOLSTEIN

WALKER & COMPANY
New York

Published by Walker Publishing Company, Inc., New York

All papers used by Walker & Company are natural, recyclable products made from wood grown in well-managed forests. The manufacturing processes conform to the environmental regulations of the country of origin.

LIBRARY OF CONGRESS CATALOGING-IN-PUBLICATION DATA

Holstein, William J.
The next American economy : blueprint for a real recovery / William J. Holstein.—1st U.S. ed.
p. cm.
Includes bibliographical references.
ISBN 978-0-8027-7750-8
1. Industries—United States—Case studies. 2. Diffusion of innovations—United States—Case studies. 3. New products—United States—Case studies. 4. Job creation—United States—Case studies. 5. Industrial policy—United States. 6. United States—Commerce. 7. United States—Economic conditions—2009– I. Title.
HC106.84.H67 2011
338.973—dc22   2010040502

Visit Walker & Company's Web site at www.walkerbooks.com

First U.S. edition 2011

1 3 5 7 9 10 8 6 4 2

Designed by Simon M. Sullivan
Typeset by Westchester Book Group
Printed in the U.S.A. by Quad/Graphics, Fairfield, Pennsylvania

CONTENTS

INTRODUCTION

The Challenge

IT IS A TIME OF DESPERATION in many quarters of the American economy. By most estimates, the United States needs to create at least 10 million to 12 million jobs to repair the damage that a devastating recession has inflicted, even if that recession is technically over. As of September 2010, some 14.9 million Americans who wished to find employment could not do so—and roughly half of them have been out of work for more than six months, a level not seen since the Great Depression in the 1930s.[1] This employment vacuum must be filled, or millions of Americans will find their living standards plummeting further downward and their American Dreams slipping into reverse. Trillions of dollars of wealth have evaporated, leaving behind a deadly pile of consumer debt and foreclosures. After a decade of scandal, from Enron's spectacular collapse to Goldman Sachs' obscene bonuses, Americans seem to have lost confidence that their institutions are working on behalf of the broader national good. One poll revealed that 61 percent of Americans believe the country is on the wrong track, up from 48 percent a year earlier.[2] In general, they have a sense that they have lost control of the nation's economic destiny. When asked about America's economic future, some cynics respond by joking darkly, "Do we have one?"

But the United States does have a future, and the heart of America's innovation engine still beats. It is not just twenty-five-year-olds coming up with Facebook applications or sleek new gadgets for Apple and Google. Americans of many ages, geographies, and industries are attempting to give birth to new industries—thin-film solar and other renewable forms of energy, simulation and modeling, advanced robotics, lithium-ion batteries, nanotechnology, biotech and genomics, and new materials, to name just a few. The creation of new industries is what America has traditionally done better than any other country in the world. From the transistor and X-ray to the Internet and biotechnology, America has always created new technologies that disrupt the established order and change the world. "The best aspect of the United States is the breadth of the thinking," says Willy C. Shih, a professor at Harvard Business School and veteran of twenty-eight years at IBM, Digital Equipment, Silicon Graphics, and Eastman Kodak. "Because of the intellectual environment, we have the most wide-open big thinkers. This is the place where you get the really far-out ideas that turn out to be important—Facebook and Google but also the transistor and the integrated circuit."[3]

The problem is that these new ideas are not taking root fast enough and aren't creating enough jobs on U.S. soil, an essential gap that economists do not understand. Many of them argue that Americans can simply wait for the economy "to get better," assuming that easy credit will flow again and Americans can return to the free-spending ways that prevailed during a prolonged financial bubble, when either stock market prices or real estate values fueled the economy and consumer spending accounted for two-thirds of all economic activity. Every time newly reported consumer spending or consumer confidence statistics are weak, these economists are disappointed. Prominent economists, including some on the White House's Council of Economic Advisers, insist that the United States needs only to wait for a turn in the business cycle—what is called a cyclical recovery.

But they are wrong to expect the economy to simply get better and wrong to expect consumer spending to reemerge as such a dominant force in the economy. If doctors misdiagnose a patient, they cannot possibly offer the right treatment. That's what mainstream economists are doing today—not recognizing the depth of the structural challenge that the U.S. economy faces as it engages with the powerhouses of East Asia. The economy needs change of a sort that will open up the valves of American innovation and create new industries, while beginning to ease the U.S. dependency on imported energy. It needs change at the microeconomic level, where Americans live, work, and shop. The goal that unites the nation should be to figure out how true wealth is created, while at the same time addressing the issue of energy dependency. Those two goals are not mutually exclusive. In fact, they are deeply connected.

It has been my life's work to study the creation of wealth from the ground up. I have been reporting and writing about it since I was a young correspondent for United Press International (UPI). After President Jimmy Carter normalized American relations with China in late 1978, UPI recognized that it needed more correspondents in Asia and assigned me to Hong Kong. Part of my job was covering nearby southern China, which emerged as ground zero in China's economic modernization efforts because it was where four special economic zones were to be built. China was an inward-looking, entirely socialist country. Vast seas of Chinese in their olive-green Mao jackets bicycled through the dark streets of the southern city of Guangzhou at night, the whirling of their wheels creating the only sounds. They were poor and had spent decades engaged in ideological struggles against each other. Now their paramount leader, Deng Xiaoping, had told them that "to get rich is glorious."

In one of the special economic zones, the Chinese wanted to build a dock to load and unload ships, but a mountain of one or two thousand feet in height blocked access to the water. Many foreign correspondents did not think the Chinese could ever break free from socialism and class struggle, but I watched thousands of Chinese laborers as they took the mountain down, stone by stone. Several dozen men were at the top with pickaxes, and then brigades of other laborers with wheelbarrows would carry the stones back down the mountain. There wasn't a single piece of mechanized equipment, not a single Caterpillar machine, to be seen. The Chinese were going to build wealth because they could focus their huge manpower on achieving a common objective— the way they were able to organize and focus their labor was their competitive advantage in a capitalist world. It was the beginning of China's emergence, and also the beginning of my understanding of the complex concept now called globalization.

The same year, I covered the economic summit of world leaders in Tokyo, which was an important milestone for Japan to stand up and be counted in the world as a major industrial power. In 1981, I stood in a remote agricultural area of Taiwan called Hsinchu and heard about grand technological plans that, of course, have now turned that area into the equivalent of a Silicon Valley. I traveled to South Korea in 1988 to chronicle the emergence of that nation as it hosted its first Olympics. That was long before the West had ever heard about Samsung or Hyundai.

Throughout this time, the impact of Asia's emergence on the lives of Americans has become increasingly evident. The first time I saw how Japan's emergence was touching Americans was when I joined *BusinessWeek* in 1985 and started traveling through my native land, particularly the Midwest and border states. It was at a time of wrenching dislocation in the American heartland as a result of the recession of 1981–82. But there was something deeper happening than just a cyclical recession. The very structure of economic activity was changing because Japanese and other foreign companies were moving in. America had been cruising along unchallenged since World War II, but now it was allowing, and indeed encouraging, globalization.

Harrodsburg, Kentucky, for example, had sent many young men to fight the Japanese in World War II in the Philippines. Twenty-nine of them died in the infamous Bataan Death March. The town had mounted a tank on the outskirts of town as a memorial to those who had fallen. Yet Hitachi Ltd., the big Japanese company, was now building an automotive electronics factory in Harrodsburg. The need for jobs was so intense that the locals overcame their historical resentments and went to work for Hitachi. American-owned companies were stumbling in global competition while Japan's companies seemed to be gaining. At the town's barber shop, Kenneth Hourigan, then seventy-three, one of the few survivors of the death march, reflected on the twist of fate. "I don't think much of it," he said, referring to the Hitachi plant. "But there ain't much I can do. They'll be accepted here eventually."[4]

Some American companies and communities were responding well to the early stirrings of globalization by learning how to export their goods to the world. That created real wealth. But most Americans were still trying to come to grips with the fact that the world had changed.

Americans soon started a national debate about their competitiveness vis-à-vis Japan. Japan was targeting specific industries such as automobiles, machine tools, semiconductors, and consumer electronics. Japan's economy was based on a very different model from China's. Japan's economy was not controlled by a monolithic Communist Party. Rather, it was organized into industrial groupings called *keiretsu*, in which members of the group cooperated in marshaling limited resources and limited technology. Toyota Motor was particularly adept in devising new manufacturing methods that represented a clear advance over prevailing American methods. Toyota's competition against General Motors did not reach a crescendo until 2009, when GM declared bankruptcy and reemerged as a smaller company. But the seeds of that competitive battle were being sown in the 1980s. During the late 1980s and early 1990s, American governments negotiated with Japan as part of such talks as the Structural Impediments Initiative in hopes of redressing a lopsided trade deficit. Those negotiations ultimately proved fruitless.

Meanwhile, the Four Tigers—Singapore, Hong Kong, Taiwan, and South Korea—were emerging. Not as sophisticated as Japan, they were nonetheless highly visible and were clearly ahead of

China. They were incredible rags-to-riches success stories, but they were so small that no Western analyst believed that they could mount an assault on global markets by themselves. What was not clear at the time was how they would become economically intertwined with Japan and, ultimately, with China.

During extended trips to Japan in 1989, researching a book, I learned a great deal more about how Japan recovered from the devastation of World War II to become the world's second-largest economy.[5] The Japanese studied how the Americans had created such strong industries, and they were in the process of calculating strategies to catch up to and surpass the West.

To be sure, a financial bubble was part of the explanation for Japan's seeming dominance. In the late 1980s, Japanese companies were buying Rockefeller Center in New York and Pebble Beach Golf Course in California, and the value of the land beneath the Imperial Palace in Tokyo was said to be worth more than all of the real estate in America. That bubble popped with real pain inflicted on Japanese banks starting in 1990, but Americans made a mistake in assuming that the underlying competitive challenge from Japan had disappeared. Overall, the competitiveness debate faded as American elites persuaded themselves that Japan had suffered a "lost decade." Americans seemed to convince themselves that if they could not force a fundamental change in Japan's strategy, they would decide that Japan no longer mattered. They would "bypass Japan." Meanwhile, on the ground, the competitive situation remained much the same: Americans gave up the consumer electronics industry and continued to suffer losses in the other sectors, as evidenced by the pressure that Toyota brought to bear on GM.

Seeking out the answers to how Americans could respond to competitive pressures, my colleagues and I at *Business Week* discovered that there were common strategies that certain parts of the United States had developed to exploit and commercialize new technologies, learning from Silicon Valley and Boston's Route 128 technology corridor.[6] These hot spots, such as Minnesota's

"Medical Alley"—home to hundreds of medical device manufacturers at the time—needed a university or a medical institution such as the Mayo Clinic to serve as idea factories to create new technologies. Then they needed the right financial support, human capital, mentoring, and other factors to allow the ideas to blossom commercially. Harvard Business School's Michael Porter chose to call these areas *clusters*, the term that ultimately prevailed.

Most recently, I wrote a book about General Motors, the largest industrial company in America.[7] The key argument in that book, and part of the genesis for this one, was that manufacturing was important to the United States as a whole. Manufacturing is where very important innovation occurs and where many high-quality jobs are created.

It was Japanese competition, not Chinese or Indian, that spotlighted flaws in GM's manufacturing processes and cost structure. Only recently have China and India, as part of the BRIC group of nations (Brazil, Russia, India, and China), come to dominate the headlines. They certainly merit the attention, not least because of their huge populations. But it has taken them decades to reach the point that Japan did in the mid-1970s and the Tigers by the 1980s. None of the previous waves of emerging nations has disappeared, as one might suspect from reading American newspapers. Japan and the Tigers have maintained their expansions, with some obvious hiccups such as the Asian financial crisis of 1997. Over time, they have been remarkably consistent and focused.

The result today is that the United States is faced with competitors that have been consciously managing their economic expansions for decades and doing it with an eye toward winning in global markets, including the United States. The fact that their strategies have been export-driven is one reason they have recovered more quickly from the most recent recession. Critics would say they have engaged in mercantilist strategies, but the Asians view them as commonsense ways to generate wealth.

Some of their success is a threat to U.S. interests, but certainly not all. Americans have been active participants in creating this system. Several U.S. administrations encouraged all this as part of *globalization*, a word with many interpretations. At heart, many American leaders have wanted economic gains to occur in this region to encourage a shift toward greater democracy and geopolitical stability, which has been a smashing success. At the same time, these leaders have assumed that Americans would be able to keep driving toward the higher, more sophisticated end of the economic ladder, to remain ahead of these emerging powers. But that sustained drive to the top has been the missing ingredient—U.S. leaders have not taken the key steps needed to ensure that the United States remains on top of the heap by creating the Next American Economy. That is why structural change is so urgently needed today.

It's not a single country that represents the challenge. The nations of East Asia have set aside bitter historical and cultural differences to engage in the pursuit of wealth. It's the combination of all these players, and a blending of their energies, that has created the broad competitive challenge. One of the analogies that Japan used to explain its aspirations in the late 1980s was a flock of geese. Japan would be the lead goose, followed by others as part of a V formation. That has largely occurred, with Hong Kong, Singapore, South Korea, and Taiwan still one step behind Japan in terms of technological sophistication. Only one of the four—South Korea—has challenged Japan's technological superiority in industries such as liquid crystal displays and autos. China is pushing very forcefully, but it's from behind all of them.

Collectively, American, European, and Japanese companies and those from the other countries of East Asia have turned China into the industrial workshop of the world. Japanese and Korean components and parts fuel much of what is assembled in China for export to the world. Taiwanese plant managers run many factories. Hong Kong supplies capital as well as distribution and marketing savvy. The Chinese portion of the profit from every

$100 worth of goods sold in America is in the range of only $10 to $30. A majority of the economic value that is added to most products is from the foreign equipment used to set up factories, the components that go into the goods, and the distribution and marketing of those goods. The ultimate example perhaps is Apple's iPod, which transformed the world of music and entertainment and earned Apple hefty profits. But the device itself is made by a Taiwanese company in China using Japanese and Korean components. Chinese prime minister Wen Jiabao was quoted as saying that workers in China earn only $6 out of the total $299 that an iPod is sold for in the United States.[8] It's much the same with iPhones and iPads. China is striving to break out of this role of simply being the workshop where others manufacture goods for the world and to emerge as a full-fledged technology-based power, but it has not yet done that—and may not be able to for many more years.

India is pursuing a very different pattern, largely at arm's length from East Asia. It is going after the full range of economic activity from information technology and software (in the form of companies such as Wipro and Infosys) to many types of manufacturing. The largest steel company in the world is owned by Lakshmi Mittal, an Indian, for example, and the Tata Group has recently bought Jaguar and Land Rover from Ford Motor, symbolizing its global aspirations.[9] It is Tata Motors, a member of the family-owned group, that produced the Nano car for roughly $2,500, attracting headlines all over the world. The Indian economic development model depends much more on nonresident Indians living in the United States, Britain, and elsewhere, rather than economic integration with Japan or the Tigers.

All these nations have concentrated on manufacturing at a time when many American companies were persuaded that all manufacturing was passé and either "outsourced" or "offshored" entire product lines. Offshoring generally means that a company moves its own manufacturing to another, less expensive country; outsourcing means that the company turns control of its manufacturing over to another company, which usually takes place in another low-cost country. In the short term, American companies profited from these trends and American consumers enjoyed an avalanche of cheap flat-screen televisions, cameras, computers, and cars. But a longer-term side effect was that the manufacturing sector in the United States was essentially hollowed out, with supplier networks and crucial engineering skills atrophying.

The fear now is that Americans will not use our own innovation to re-create and expand our manufacturing base. Professor Shih, an American-born Chinese who moves easily between East and West and who in many ways encapsulates the debate about America's technological strengths, notes that U.S. researchers tend to be very good at systematic thinking, meaning that they integrate diverse technologies and diverse ideas.[10] But Shih argues that the Americans have allowed their industrial *commons* to deteriorate in recent years. By that term, he means the supplier base, toolmakers, and the labor and engineering pools—"all that stuff you tap into when you're trying to put together a company to make something."

Those are precisely the capabilities that Japan, China, Taiwan, South Korea, Singapore, and others have consciously targeted through a combination of government policies such as tax breaks and strong engineering educational programs. Executives of East Asian companies tend to look at the United States as a "research funnel"—a source of ideas they can commercialize. Shih recalls having dinner with the CEO of a Korean company, who told him, "You guys are very good at the front-end R&D. We'll just take all that stuff and commercialize it and we'll make all the money." Shih adds ruefully: "Even though we have the primary technology, there is a lot involved in manufacturing these things at a reasonable cost. That's where Asians have the lead."

What should be done? Some policy makers seem to hold out hope that Washington will persuade the Chinese to take further steps to revalue their currency and that will take care of all of the U.S. competitive challenges. But the Americans have lost the political power to force Japan or China to fundamentally reorder their economic priorities. Those nations own too much of the U.S. government's debt and will not be lectured to by the country whose policies precipitated an international financial meltdown.

The fact is that China, a nation of 1.3 billion, is determined to become an economic superpower. The missionary era of urging the Asians to recognize the superiority of Western ways is over. Instead, Americans should be concentrating on what we can control, which is how we organize the U.S. economy and the institutions that make it up at the microeconomic level. That would allow us to "ride the dragon" of Asia's economic emergence, not passively stand in the way and be overrun.

Many Americans express concern that there is no way to "defeat" the Asians. But we don't have to beat the Asians and probably cannot. With half the world's population, the very different countries that Westerners lump together as "Asia" outnumber Americans by a ten-to-one margin. China alone outnumbers America by more than four to one. The United States does not *have* to be the world's largest economy. The goal should be to possess the highest per capita income, the strongest technology base, and the highest living standards. The goal, in short, should be to dominate the high end of the economic food chain. This is precisely the strategy that Japan has adopted as it watches the emergence of China next door. The Japanese know that the Chinese are in the process of dislodging them as the second-largest economy in the world, but they will fight to maintain a huge advantage in per capita income and overall wealth. Their companies possess commanding technological leads over any would-be Chinese competitors. And the Japanese economy is about ten times as large as China's on a per capita basis because it has only one-tenth as many people, suggesting a huge advantage in prosperity. Flying from China to Japan, or vice versa, one is struck by how the Japanese have maintained their living standards and the sophistication of their public infrastructure over those of the mainland despite China's rapid development of airports, high-speed rail links, and highways.

The alternative to riding the dragon, as Japan is doing, is stark: The United States plays the role of a less advanced society, providing agricultural, metal, and wood products in exchange for more sophisticated goods made elsewhere. Ultimately, Americans have to ask what kind of economy we want for ourselves and our children. Do we wish to accept an economy in which we send our children to work in the factories of non-American firms and allow the design and engineering to be done in Japan, Korea, China, and Europe? No. Our goal should be to have a high percentage of value-added jobs in engineering, design, finance, computerization, marketing, and similar fields. These depend on innovation and manufacturing.

There are tangible steps that American businesses, governments, educational institutions, companies, and individuals should now be taking to create long-term, sustainable wealth for the United States as a whole, not just for Wall Street elites. The tools and the knowledge exist to achieve a real economic recovery.

Politicians shouting "Jobs, jobs, jobs" in Washington do not seem to have a deep understanding of how the private sector creates jobs. They are mesmerized by the political game and by trying to jockey for votes by, say, extending unemployment insurance, which is a mere Band-Aid.

Economists, for their part, do not understand the ecosystems that create wealth because they rarely allow their tasseled loafers to set foot on the ground outside their ivory towers, relying instead on data that appear on their computer monitors. They are highly visible on television talking about the gross national product and the rate at which it increases or decreases, or whether it's time for the Federal Reserve to raise interest rates. But their macroeconomic tools don't equip them to understand where wealth comes from and how to make it sustainable over the long term. As macroeconomists, they don't understand what happens at the micro level.

Moreover, too many economists are pushing isms. One may be a Keynesian, another may be a University of Chicago free marketeer, yet another may be a Ronald Reagan supply-sider. These ideologies do not create national wealth. Wealth creation should be completely nonideological, just as the Japanese and Chinese have discovered. Some things work; others don't. Grand theories should be checked at the front door.

The intellectual models that most economists use also are based on a single national economy, but we now live in a truly globalized economy where trade and investment do not halt at the water's edge. Many of the analytical tools economists use are grossly out of date, having been invented in the 1930s, '40s, and '50s. Take the concept of capacity utilization, which purports to measure how busy American factories are and hence the inflationary pressures facing the economy as a whole. This concept was invented at a time when steel was the primary output of American factories, long before the computer or semiconductor were invented and long before the rise of a vital service sector. The economy has been transformed, yet some of the tools being used to describe it have not been modernized.

Too many economists also don't understand the *quality* of economic activity. To them, a person making $15 an hour dealing cards at a casino is generating the same output as one on a manufacturing line producing goods that command a strong position in the U.S. and world markets. One job requires relatively low levels of education and is highly vulnerable to the vagaries of the tourist economy; the other requires real skills and can be defended against international competition. One type of job, and industry, is ephemeral; the other is sustainable because it has a competitive advantage.

What we are now waking up to as a society is that many of the forms of wealth that America has pursued are proving not to be defensible. Building casinos in Las Vegas, erecting deluxe housing complexes and luxury condominiums on speculation, and creating vast strip malls where people borrow money from China to buy an abundance of things they don't really need (also made in China)—none of that is ultimately as sustainable as we once thought. Nor are investment bankers creating real wealth when they use more financial leverage to create ever more exotic investment instruments.

One reason the current economic challenge is so severe is that the United States lived in a kind of fool's paradise during the bubble years and did not take concerted action to defend its standard of living from an across-the-board competitive challenge and also did not respond adequately to the energy challenge. In the vernacular, we've been hit by a triple whammy—the end of easy money, increasingly powerful global competition, and a failure to ease our dependence on imported energy.

Part of the explanation is the failure of ideology, dating back to 1980 and Ronald Reagan's presidency. For thirty years we believed Reagan's mantra that trade and fiscal deficits did not matter. It was fine to buy all the oil we needed from the Middle East because we just sent those countries little pieces of green paper called dollars, and it was acceptable to buy all our cars, televisions, and consumer electronics from Japan, South Korea, and China because, again, we were simply sending them pieces of paper. We didn't think it made any difference which countries held those dollars because we assumed they would have to reinvest them in U.S. capital markets, the richest, deepest, and most transparent in the world. It didn't make any difference who controlled those dollars, or so we thought. Ownership of dollars was "neutral." This free market ideology urged Americans to let the "invisible hand" of the market do its work, almost magically, as suggested long ago by economist Adam Smith.

But a monumental loss of wealth has demonstrated the shortcomings of this ideology. Now it's time to start digging out. As the immensity of the challenge becomes clearer, at least some Americans will be eager to examine the origins of how wealth is really created for their communities and states, and for their nation as a whole.

This book is about real Americans doing real things, right

now. Part one offers case studies about places and people involved in creating technology clusters. Central to each is the role of idea factories, whether they are universities, corporate laboratories, or national weapons labs, as places where Americans create world-class ideas. For example, lithium-ion batteries are expected to be used widely in hybrid and electric vehicles, as well as in devices that store solar and wind energy as part of "smart" electricity grids. Americans are behind in this sector, but chapter one introduces a technology champion in the form of A123 Systems, of Watertown, Massachusetts, which used nanophosphate technology from the Massachusetts Institute of Technology (MIT) to create high-power lithium-ion batteries. A123 has started building a new factory in Michigan. A new industry is being born amid the ashes left behind by decades of destruction in the auto industry.

Borrowing some of the lessons from Boston and Silicon Valley, Pittsburgh has created a cluster of forty different advanced robotics companies, many associated with Carnegie Mellon University (chapter two). They are working on vehicles that drive themselves, and on deploying robots to conduct minimally invasive surgery on the heart and other parts of the human body, distribute drugs in hospital pharmacies, operate warehouses, and inspect the nation's aging infrastructure of sewers and water lines. These robotic systems represent a technological leapfrog over Japanese robots that function only repetitively in a stable environment, as in the paint shop of an auto factory. The next generation of robots can "sense" their environment and make autonomous decisions.

The emergence of Orlando's simulation and training cluster (chapter three) has been spurred by the Department of Defense, which spends $5 billion a year there on hardware and software. Some one hundred simulation companies also have taken advantage of the presence of Disney and Universal, and a major office of Electronic Arts, to create programs that borrow liberally from entertainment and the computer gaming industry. Their products are aimed at helping the military train tens of thousands of new recruits each year to fight in Iraq and Afghanistan. But many of the companies, such as Productivity Apex and IDEAS, are using their business with the military and the National Aeronautics and Space Administration (NASA) to launch products for the civilian economy in education, medicine, and logistics. If they are successful, these companies could create tens of thousands of jobs—and their products could result in huge productivity gains for the whole economy.

The military does not completely dominate innovation, of course. San Diego has enjoyed the remarkable rise of its biotechnology cluster, thanks in part to funding from the National Institutes of Health (NIH). The once sleepy navy town has become a world leader in the emerging field of genomics, a blend of life sciences and massive computing power (chapter four). Corning's development of Gorilla Glass for the consumer electronics industry (chapter five) was driven completely by the needs of the commercial marketplace. The company noticed that the owners of mobile telephones and other handheld devices were frustrated because their devices broke so easily after being dropped. The company, located in the upstate New York town that bears its name, dug into its treasure trove of glass formulations and found a superhard glass product it had tried unsuccessfully to introduce in 1962 for the automotive market. No other company in the world has a competitive product. This is an example of how a major U.S. company relies on its own internal resources to innovate.

Will new industries, by themselves, create 10 million to 12 million jobs? Almost certainly not. But they are producing some of the highest-quality jobs, meaning they are defensible against the vagaries of Wall Street and the hot money that once coursed through the housing and stock markets. They are also the most sustainable against global competition.

Part two offers case studies about cities or regions that have created ecosystems of the future as part of a broad push to increase the sophistication of the U.S. economy. The American effort to rebound must also include a structural change in the U.S. dependence on imported energy, which is what Austin, Texas, is trying to achieve (chapter six). The Next American Economy requires a higher level of sophistication in exporting, and North Carolina has developed a strong ecosystem to promote exports from small companies, including a surprising number of high-technology firms (chapter seven). Other key elements of a real recovery are encouraging chief executive officers of large companies to locate more of their research and manufacturing on U.S. soil, as NCR has done in Atlanta (chapter eight). A final case study demonstrates how Cleveland is successfully using a community college to retrain the American workforce (chapter nine). If we cannot create the right skill sets, the industries of the future will take root in China and Malaysia and South Korea.

From these case studies, part three extracts tangible lessons. A common theme is that Americans must work across traditional institutional boundaries to create climates of cooperation. In response to the conscious, long-term competitive strategies that other nations are deploying, Americans also need greater institutional coherence.

Chapter ten draws conclusions about how local and regional alliances should pursue that goal. Chapter eleven concentrates on prescriptions for the federal government, which does not yet have a coherent, focused industrial policy. Chapter twelve argues that chief executive officers of large American companies should not overlook the advantages of maintaining a strong presence on U.S. soil. A final chapter offers the American people straight talk about what changes we need to make to respond to the economic challenges the country faces. Too many do not understand that there are clear, practical steps we can take every day to defend our way of life and to secure a brighter economic future.

PART I

★ ★ ★

TECHNOLOGY CLUSTERS

ONE

MIT and A123 Systems

How Innovation Happens in a Premier Hot Spot

Ric Fulop, a twenty-six-year-old serial entrepreneur originally from Venezuela, was looking for a new idea in early
2001 to create his sixth company. He approached the technology licensing office at the Massachusetts Institute of Technology
in Cambridge, Massachusetts, which had licensed technology to
him for a previous company. "My next start-up is going to be a
battery start-up," he told tech officials. "Whom should I go see?"[1]

Fulop was pushing a carbon nanotube notion, and the MIT
officials thought that would be of interest to Professor Yet-Ming
Chiang, who had displayed interest in commercializing technologies from his lab. They knew he had just filed a statement
with the tech office announcing that he had achieved a promising breakthrough on what he thought was a revolutionary new
self-organizing battery.

At their recommendation, Fulop knocked on the professor's
door just as Chiang was preparing to leave for a battery conference and told him he wanted to launch a new business on the
basis of the nanotube idea. Chiang, however, told him that he
had a better idea.[2] After returning from his conference, the professor called a colleague, Bart Riley, who was working at American Superconductor at the time. Riley recalls Chiang's first
description of Fulop: "I met this crazy guy who walked into my
office and said he's starting a company, but you have to meet
him too."

Chiang's father was born in mainland China but escaped in 1948 in front of the advancing Communists and fled to Taiwan, where he became a train engineer for the Taiwan Sugar Company. Young Chiang arrived in Brooklyn at age six without speaking English. In one of those classic tales of young immigrants making huge advances, he went on to become an American citizen at age sixteen and earn a PhD from MIT in materials science.

Chiang and Riley—who also has a PhD in materials science—started meeting with Fulop. Their project was secret because they did not want anyone else to discover what technology they were considering. They created their company in November 2001 and chose the name A123 Systems, which comes from the obscure Hamaker force constant used to describe how the self-organizing battery would work.

Fulop was instrumental in attracting the first venture capital money, the so-called A round. Some $8.3 million came from North Bridge Venture Partners, YankeeTech, and Sequoia. Also putting up money was Gururaj "Desh" Deshpande, founder of Cascade Communications and Sycamore Networks. Deshpande's role would prove to be very important because he joined the board as chairman and served as an adviser and mentor for the team. Motorola and Qualcomm added $4 million shortly thereafter. Qualcomm's chairman and CEO, Paul Jacobs, would join the A123 board, giving it more credibility and experience.

Chiang didn't halt his research into other ideas, maintaining one foot in the business world and one in academe. At about this time, A123 received a $100,000 Small Business Innovation Research (SBIR) grant from the Small Business Administration, in cooperation with the U.S. Department of Energy, that helped the company start commercializing a completely different idea that also originated in Chiang's MIT lab. This was for new materials for the cathodes in batteries in hybrid electric vehicles.

It wasn't clear that A123 needed a full-time CEO at this point because they did not truly have a product and had only five employees. But they knew that they would need a seasoned business leader who could help the company grow, a skill set that none of the founders possessed. The three cofounders found just the man—Dave Vieau, who had worked for Texas Instruments starting in 1972. He had worked most recently at American Power Conversion for about ten years as vice president of marketing and sales before running a series of small start-ups. In short, he had spent several decades managing companies, large and small, and had a successful track record. "We all felt Dave was the right guy," Chiang recalls.

Chiang's academic research continued. In September 2002, he published a paper on nanophosphates in *Nature Materials*. The company organized a small team to evaluate this technology, but it was still on the back burner.

Riley, as chief technology officer and vice president in charge of R&D, took responsibility for Chiang's original technique for making a self-organizing battery that relied on dispersing materials into a container and allowing the particles to organize themselves into a network. That would drastically reduce the costs of manufacturing a battery. MIT granted an exclusive license to the technology in exchange for an ownership stake in the company and a royalty stream if the company ever became successful. It did not ask for a big up-front payment of any sort. This policy is one of the reasons so many companies have been created by MIT professors or students.

A123 had about fifteen employees at this point, in the spring of 2003, but engineers who had been hired to work on the self-organizing battery idea confronted the founders of the company and told them the idea would never "scale" in time. It just wasn't practical. CEO Vieau called a meeting, and all the employees sat together at a table and promised each other that they were not going to leave until they had forced a decision. Two cofounders of the company—Riley and Chiang—were being told, in effect, their original idea faced too many technical challenges.

It was at that point that the company, with its board's agreement, shifted to the second idea that Chiang was working on at

MIT—the nanophosphate technology that could be used in lithium-ion batteries. Traditional phosphates did not have high energy or power levels but were considered relatively safe in batteries.

What Chiang had done was to modify the structure of the phosphate using nanotechnology, meaning he made the particles even smaller. He also "doped" it—in layman's terms, he revved it up—to improve its performance. The company believed this new powderized material would allow for safer, lighter, more powerful batteries that could be discharged and recharged more times over their lifetime. "We were riding two horses for a while, but we killed the first horse and rode off on the second one," recalls Vieau.[3]

This flexibility was unusual because most founders of a company would insist that their first vision was right. "If an idea is not working well, people typically dig in, and dig in until they fail," Vieau adds. The presence of an experienced business leader, with a seasoned board of directors, helped the founders adjust to a new reality.

The policies that a university puts into place to foster commercialization of ideas are hugely important, as the case of A123 demonstrates. MIT professors are encouraged to spend one day a week doing something other than pure academics. They can get time off to pursue their ideas, as much as a year. At many universities in the United States and around the world, professors can't do any of that. They must stay in academia full-time or leave. It's black or white. The fact that someone such as Chiang can move back and forth gracefully between the two worlds helps strengthen the connection between the laboratory and the commercial marketplace.

The role of the technology licensing office is also critical. MIT was one of the first major universities to take advantage of the Bayh-Dole Act of 1980, also called the Small Business Patent Procedures Act. This law, enacted in the waning days of the

Carter administration, is an example of a piece of legislation that does not attract much attention when it is passed but proves to be enormously powerful. Prior to this act, the U.S. government owned all the patents that universities filed for because government dollars had supported their research. But only 5 percent of those patents had actually been put to commercial use. With this act, the government agreed that universities or institutes owned the intellectual property and could license it or transfer it to private companies.

The way this process works today at MIT is that professors alert the technology licensing office about promising research discoveries by filing "disclosures." The office gets five hundred disclosures a year. It evaluates them, decides what to seek a patent for, and then hires outside patent attorneys to actually file for the patents. It is expensive work but necessary.

The office also serves as a matchmaker between researchers and the world of seasoned business managers and investors. The philosophy that guides the office is clear. "The question is how we can get real contributions to the economy as opposed to letting professors play in their sandboxes working on things that seem completely irrelevant," says Lita Nelsen, director of the office. "Yes, we want them to work on blue-sky research, but we also want to take the by-products of that basic research and make it useful."[4] Blue-sky research means pushing the cutting edge of knowledge rather than seeking commercial application for a technology.

The federal government's role in supporting the creation of ideas at MIT, as at many universities, is central. Academics obtain government grants for much of their research—whether from the National Science Foundation, the Department of Energy, the military's Defense Advanced Research Projects Agency (DARPA), the U.S. Air Force, NASA, or others. "Without federal funding, this whole thing goes away," Nelsen says. Industry labs such as Bell Labs, Xerox PARC, and IBM Research Laboratories have either disappeared or had their budgets cut over the years, and they tended to concentrate on applied research, also called development research, more so than blue-sky research. This is one of the most important debates about U.S. government support for research: To what extent should it support scientists who are pushing the edge of knowledge, and to what extent should it fund applied research that might create specific products for the market-place?

However the money is allocated, it's clear there's a limit on what federal funding can achieve, meaning Washington cannot just wave a magic wand and create high-paying jobs by fund-ing R&D. At some point the private sector has to take over the funding of start-ups—and that is easier to achieve in a cluster because of the concentration of both human and financial capi-tal. MIT's formal and informal networks are advanced in how they put knowledgeable investors in touch with researchers. In-vestors, for example, sometimes come give lectures in the class-room so that they can meet professors and students. The university boasts a venture mentoring service, student clubs, and competi-tions that recognize the best business ideas, all essential lubri-cants. The Deshpande Center for Technological Innovation is attempting to serve as a bridge between academics and investors to make sure that promising ideas are developed.[5] And the nearby presence of the MIT Sloan School of Management facilitates the introduction of scientists to business-minded students.

When it comes time to link scientists with private capital, Nelsen does not believe that angel funds from investors with nontechnical backgrounds are the best source because those in-dividuals probably have never started companies and cannot offer practical advice. "That's the wrong kind of angel," in her view. Academics with a hot idea need investors such as Desh-pande, who has successfully created companies and is committed to a company's success over the long run. His type of venture capitalism is very different from that of venture capitalists (VCs) who seek to make their exit from a company after only eighteen months or two years and often pressure management to pump up earnings and stock price in the short run at the expense of long-term performance.

So even though the federal government is important, the vast majority of the money needed to commercialize new ideas comes from the private sector, and the majority of that needs to be purchases of equity, not grants. "It has to be balanced," says Nelsen. "You can't just give people money." Merely giving grants does not encourage the entrepreneurs to become truly independent; in some ways, that encourages dependence.

Her office does not insist on big up-front payments from professors or students trying to start companies because that obviously would discourage them. Nor does it seek to control the companies, which some universities do. Understanding the proper balance between the university and the private sector seems to be key. "We are not a venture capitalist," Nelsen explains. "We are the people who have the intellectual property. To spare the company from high costs, we take very modest up-front costs and low-single-digit percentages of shares."

In some ways, what Nelsen's office does is like buying a lottery ticket. Perhaps seventy to eighty companies get started each year with technology licensed by her office, but only a few will emerge as winners. "Our philosophy is to get a bunch of them started and let the market and investors decide how the company should be run," she explains.

The fact that MIT has been doing this for generations means that its systems have matured. "It's been going on for fifty years," she says. "We call it the entrepreneurial ecosystem. Some organisms come in and grow; others don't grow. And they interact virally. There is no supervisory body." That is a central insight—no one is in charge, not the university, not the entrepreneurs, not investors, not major companies. The different institutions and individuals have to collaborate and find common interests. This is the heart of how America's idea factories engage with the larger economy around them.

After its abrupt change in direction in early 2003, A123 was awarded another Department of Energy/SBIR grant of $750,000 to demonstrate that it could manufacture a battery cathode with its nanophosphate powder. It was able to do that at a Motorola plant in Georgia. The larger company's support was critical. A123 also started experimenting by turning to a Korean company to actually coat the electrodes with the powder. The electrodes are combined to create battery cells, which ultimately are put together into larger systems. A123 also turned to a Taiwanese subcontractor to make its battery cells, which are combined to make battery packs. It farmed out the work in this manner partly to stretch its own funding but also to prevent any competitor from discovering its technological secrets. It kept developing its product through 2003 and 2004 and was able to raise $20 million by selling shares in June 2004.

A123's first real customer was Black & Decker, which wanted lighter, more powerful batteries for its handheld tools. When newspapers started writing about Black & Decker's launch of its 36-volt tools in November 2005, using batteries from A123, it was the end of A123's "stealth" period.

Problem was, A123 could not build enough factories, fast enough, to supply Black & Decker with all that it wanted, a common problem facing start-ups. "We didn't know whether we could meet the price or the time deadline," says Riley.[6] To get the job done, he set up a system in which A123 made its nanophosphate powder and shipped it to South Korea, where a Korean partner coated the powder onto metal foil, the next step in assembling a lithium-ion battery.

Then the coated electrodes were shipped to China, where they were assembled into cells, before being shipped to Taiwan, where ten cells were combined into a battery pack. They were then shipped to Black & Decker's factory in Mexico. "You should see my passport," Riley jokes. Now forty-six, he made long international journeys every month for two to three years.

It required strong connections among Chiang and the other principals because they spent years together, in what entrepreneurs call the "valley of death," without knowing for sure whether they would be successful. Chiang retained the title of founder and served as a visionary for the technology but did not assume a day-to-day management role.

In 2006, A123 concluded its business with Black & Decker, but it kept building momentum and credibility for its underlying technology, one building block at a time. It announced it would develop battery modules for fuel cell hybrid buses with General Electric.

By this point, it was increasingly up to Vieau to guide the company's strategy. He had hired a chief financial officer and other business-only executives to create the infrastructure that ultimately would attract more capital. None of the founders really knew how to do that. Scale was particularly important because A123 was up against large Japanese, Korean, and Chinese battery companies in particular, all of which had enjoyed a head start and could throw around hundreds of millions of dollars on technology or manufacturing capacity. Vieau estimates that any company that wants to compete in lithium-ion batteries has to raise $1 billion just as an ante to join the poker game.

The year 2009 was the breakout year for A123, some eight years after its founding. The arrival of the Obama administration was one factor because the new president was committed to fostering green industries as one way of responding to U.S. dependence on oil imported from all over the world and from some governments that were either not stable or not sympathetic to U.S. values.[7] A123 was able to argue that it deserved incentives to establish manufacturing in the United States so that the country would not merely substitute dependence on Chinese clean energy for dependence on Middle Eastern oil.

Sensing the new political tone, GE stepped up its commitment to A123 in April 2009 with fresh investment dollars and by taking a seat on the company's board. General Motors decided not to use A123's technology for the Chevrolet Volt, at least not yet, and instead tapped LG Chem of South Korea. For its part, Ford Motor turned to Johnson Controls Power Solutions to supply it with lithium-ion technology licensed from SAFT of France. In both GM's and Ford's cases, their cells would be made offshore and brought to U.S. factories to be assembled into packs. The American auto industry, in short, was relying on lithium-ion technology controlled by other nations.

A123, however, announced it would build a plant to make its batteries on U.S. soil and locate the full technological chain in America. That set off a scramble among U.S. states competing for the plant, and Michigan was clearly the most aggressive, sending a team of investment officials to Boston to talk to A123. They won the bidding by offering more than $100 million in tax credits, grants, and low-interest loans. Michigan also made the most sense as a location because that's where the American-owned car industry is based and it also offered large numbers of skilled tradesmen and engineers because of the upheaval that has hit GM, Ford, and Chrysler. The state agreed to retrain workers, another critical ingredient of A123's decision. Plus millions of square feet of cheap manufacturing space were available. The company chose a site in Livonia, in suburban Detroit.

In August, A123 received $249 million in clean energy monies from the Obama administration and then went public on September 24, 2009, under the ticker symbol AONE. Going public is a huge step because this is how privately held start-up companies tap into the much larger public markets, where much more capital is available. The market capitalization of A123 (the number of shares times the value of each share) soared as high as $2.8 billion before settling back to $1.6 billion. This created real wealth for many people, including the many A123 employees who held shares. Overall, Vieau says the company raised slightly less than $500 million from governments and $400 million from the IPO, plus other money from private investors, giving the company the $1 billion scale to compete. It now clearly will survive even though it is not expected to make a profit until 2011.

In short, A123 Systems is now the American leader in lithium-ion batteries—an entirely different technology from what the company started with. Lithium-ion batteries are poised to become a multibillion-dollar industry as auto companies, electricity utilities, and others turn to the new technology. AllianceBernstein estimates that sales of lithium-ion batteries could amount to $150 billion by 2030 globally.

The company has more than sixteen hundred employees in the United States and Asia, with 2009 sales of $91 million. Its factory in Michigan will create hundreds more well-paying jobs. In short, it is creating real wealth. "This is the kind of opportunity that people historically come to America for," says Chiang, today fifty-one. "This is the American Dream."

The reality is that for every A123 that is born and reaches for profitability, dozens of others fail. And for every disruptive technology that is commercialized, dozens remain locked inside academia.

But A123 overcame huge obstacles. It had no business leadership at first, started with a technology that ultimately did not work, gave itself a name that didn't correspond to the technology that emerged as its key product, and lacked the ability to actually make its product in sufficient volume. Yet the company has blossomed.

How is that possible? The keys appear to have been the ecosystem that MIT and venture capitalists had established, federal government funding at key moments, strong technology, cohesiveness among the management team, and an open climate toward immigration of talented people from around the world. Attention from larger companies—Motorola, Qualcomm, and GE—lent the company credibility and helped it manage the issues of growth.

Vieau, fifty-nine, proved to be an unusual business leader because, after managing several large businesses, he chose to devote his energies to a start-up. The common perception is that executives of large companies are not able to function in a start-up environment, but Vieau was able to guide the company through several different stages of commercialization.

Another important player was Deshpande, chairman of the board and an early investor. Having been through the creation of two companies himself, he could offer wise counsel to Vieau and others. Whenever the company stumbled, Deshpande understood how tricky new technologies can be. "Boards can react in different ways," Vieau says. They can either fire top management or help them work through the challenges.

Was A123's emergence an example of industrial policy? Obviously, yes. The U.S. government, under both Democrats and Republicans, invested in A123 over the years. The U.S. Advanced Battery Consortium, funded by large automakers and the government, also helped A123. And the state of Michigan helped lure its new plant, helping ensure that the entire technological chain of making lithium-ion batteries would be located on U.S. soil.

Critics of industrial policy would argue that the government engaged in picking winners and losers, which it definitely did. But it happened to be smart industrial policy rather than pork barrel industrial policy, which just benefits a handful of interest groups. It was also smart because the policy did not squander government resources on technology that never materializes and never creates jobs.

Vieau argues that government support was essential. "The country needs to solve both the jobs problem and the energy dependence problem, which is outrageous," he says. "We have a hundred-year problem in terms of dependence."

Lithium-ion batteries won't solve that problem alone, and it will take years before they account for a significant percentage of U.S. energy use, but they represent a start. They are not some sort of magical solution, because they will require electricity to recharge, and that could put pressures on the electricity grid in some parts of the country at some times of the day. But surely they will ease dependence on oil from Saudi Arabia, Nigeria, Venezuela, and elsewhere. "I don't think we as Americans need to participate in all forms of manufacturing, but energy is one where we do," Vieau says. "Right now, we buy $350 billion worth of foreign oil a year. That's damaging our dollar. That's damaging our economic infrastructure. Our money is going away."

The United States was once an "innovation engine," Vieau argues, but it has allowed that capability to erode, in part by outsourcing so much manufacturing to other countries. Now it needs to claw back some lost territory. "We should create the ideas and we should turn them into industries," he says. Against all odds, that's what A123 has done.

★ ★ ★

TWO

From Steel to Advanced Robots
Pittsburgh Attempts to Reinvent

PITTSBURGH'S SKIES WERE ONCE DARK with soot from steel mills, which turned out steel to build the railroads across America and supplied defense contractors and automakers for decades. But today there is not a single steel mill left, reflecting the bitter shakeout that transformed the industry. Pittsburgh also was once a major headquarters city for companies such as Gulf & Western, Westinghouse, and Alcoa, but several of those are gone too, whether sold or simply relocated. Wave after wave of industrial transformation means that Pittsburgh is a city that has suffered.

The challenge for Pittsburgh was not to create a brand-new industry in a new Sunbelt place, which seems easy in comparison, but rather to create new industries in an older city with a proud tradition. The city built a major educational sector around Carnegie Mellon University and the University of Pittsburgh and its medical services are nationally recognized, hence the local joke that the city has concentrated on "eds and meds." Finance remains a bedrock industry for the city, so the service sector has been one key to the city's ability to rebound. The Group of 20 diplomatic summit held in Pittsburgh was testament to the fact that the city has done a much better job of rejuvenating itself than, say, Detroit.

But the ultimate goal for this town is to create a new manufacturing industry, namely, advanced robotics. Carnegie Mellon, located in the Oakland district, just east of downtown, is clearly at the center of the drive to create that industry. About thirty-five to forty robotics companies—with names such as Aethon, Cardiorobotics, Automatica, Dragon Runner, Bossa Nova, Hyperactive Technologies, and Mobile Fusion—have sprung up in Pittsburgh itself or in outlying suburbs. Many took their inspiration from Carnegie Mellon.

Pittsburgh has not yet spawned a Dell or a Hewlett-Packard, partly because robotics is such a complex technical field and is still relatively young, but also because Pittsburgh's culture seems to have been shaped by the years of loss. The competition among universities and departments within the universities for funding is sharp. Government agencies, nonprofits, and foundations, established during a previous era of greater prosperity, seem to compete to define their roles and don't coordinate as smoothly as they might. There isn't as much venture capital financing for entrepreneurs as there is in Silicon Valley or Boston or Austin, and one does not feel the same sense of optimism as newer cities boast.

How then can Carnegie Mellon do a better job of pushing ideas out into the economy, and how can Pittsburgh's ecosystem of financing and business formation best support the growth of larger innovative enterprises?

The academic equivalent of a rock star at Carnegie Mellon is William L. "Red" Whittaker.[1] His office is downstairs in a building named in part for Herbert Simon, an early leader in artificial intelligence who won a Nobel Prize in 1978. Whittaker is head of the Field Robotics Center in the School of Computer Science. At sixty-one, he's bald, but his nickname persists. "I used to have hair, and it used to be red," he jokes.[2]

Whittaker designed and built the robots that went into the Three Mile Island nuclear power plant after it suffered a partial meltdown in 1984 to clean up the radioactive mess. He built three machines, and one made it into the flooded basement of the containment building and remediated the problem. No human being ever entered. Whittaker is legendary for this feat; the circle of computer, software, and robotics people who helped him accomplish this describe themselves to visitors by saying, "I was the second person Red called" or "I was the fourth." It was from this experience that he conceived of the idea of the Field Robotics Center, and he has created robotic vehicles that work in abandoned coal mines, enter live volcanoes, and search Antarctica for meteorites. He also built the robots that entered the ill-fated Chernobyl nuclear power plant in what was the Soviet Union.

Another exploit was creating a vehicle that could drive itself. The U.S. Defense Advanced Research Projects Agency sponsored a competition among universities starting in 2004 to see who could create a vehicle that could navigate its own way as part of a contest called the Grand Challenge. At the time, Whittaker recalls that critics said it was "ludicrous. Can't be done. It's not the time. Maybe in the future." He keeps ticking off the criticisms he heard: "The technology won't work. The time isn't right. It costs too much. It's not my job. Not in my factory."

Whittaker's team competed in the race in 2004 and 2005; no team won the first race, and Stanford University won it in 2005. Licking his wounds, Whittaker continued to receive support from Caterpillar and General Motors, and his team kept working on the vehicle, which they tested on the grounds of a former steel mill on one of Pittsburgh's rivers. That location symbolized the challenge: moving from steel to robotics.

The next time the race was held in 2007, this time in the desert east of Los Angeles and this time called the Urban Challenge, one of the team's two self-driving Chevrolet Tahoes won by driving 55 miles completely unassisted by human hands. They won $2 million from DARPA. "When people look at me, winning the Urban Challenge," Whittaker reflects, "what they miss is how much losing I did on the way to winning and that it took more than twelve hundred days."

Now he wants to put a robot on the moon. Google, which has a large presence in Pittsburgh because of its base of computer-related skills, is offering $25 million to the first group that can put a robotic vehicle on the moon by 2012, travel 500 meters to the historic landing site of Apollo 11, and transmit video images back to Earth. It is called the Google Lunar X Prize. Whittaker is pondering how to send a robotic vehicle to the moon and how to equip it with a power source that can endure a hard cryogenic freeze, which happens on the parts of the moon that are not facing the sun.

Altogether, he's been pursuing his vision of advanced robotics for thirty years. Advances in all the fields that support advanced robots—such as semiconductors, software, lasers, and optics—mean that robotics is now "a sure bet," he argues. "There's no turning back. It wasn't like it was twenty-five years ago, when it would have been the stuff of fantasy and science fiction, not fact. When a technology is crawling out of the primeval ooze, it isn't at all apparent that it's going to make it. But I will assert that the technical revolution of this era is that robots achieved mobility by combining new navigation capability with locomotion."

Robots have long been deployed in industrial settings, but they mostly do things such as spray-painting cars and stuffing transistors into circuit boards. They make repetitive movements, time and time again, in a controlled, stationary environment. "That's a class of robotics that is bolted to the factory floor," Whittaker says with obvious disdain. He envisions that mobile robots can transform mining, defense (flying drones already have altered the nature of the conflict against Taliban and Al-Qaeda leaders), agriculture, and automobiles. "These are unstoppable movements," he adds.

Whittaker is steeped in knowledge of how technology has changed the world—how Charles Lindbergh proved that it was possible to fly from New York to Paris and how researchers at Carnegie Mellon helped prove that a computer could beat a human chess master in 1997. He also knows how global positioning systems (GPS) have transformed the vehicles that millions of Americans drive. "At the time scientists came up with that idea, the constellation of satellites was not in the sky," he explains. "To the extent they were, you needed rack-mounted receivers to get the three or four signals. Satellites were only in view for perhaps twenty minutes a day. You could only determine location, statically, within a city block. What's this idea that it could be useful to guiding a vehicle?" Of course, GPS navigational systems can now pinpoint a moving vehicle with great accuracy.

What is it about Carnegie Mellon that allows someone such as Whittaker to pursue what he calls a "movement" to change the world? "I chose Pittsburgh for this robotics initiative," he recalls. "I was looking for a setting that had everything under one roof. I needed a region with a very technical base. What was needed to build a movement were the technical ingredients that included mechanisms, electronics, and computing with the software that goes with it. Computing was the wild card. Maybe it would make it, maybe it wouldn't, anywhere in the world." It's hard to believe now, but in the late 1970s, it was not clear that computers would ever truly emerge.

Grouping the different academic disciplines together is part of the answer. But there's also been a very rich "crossroads" effect at Carnegie Mellon because of the presence of large outside players such as DARPA and NASA from government and General Motors and Caterpillar from the private sector. They inform Whittaker and his researchers about what the needs of the outside world might be. The students, coming from so many different nations and cultures, are another part of the mix; Whittaker acknowledges that sometimes he merely harnesses their energy and ambition. "Behind every development there are great people, in my experience—a few breakthrough players and an outstanding leader," Whittaker says. "The crossroads and cross-pollination of energy and ideas and infrastructure is key."

Whittaker does not think the same kind of creative stew exists in Japan because the Japanese lack the ability to allow ideas to bubble up from young researchers, which is a sharp contrast with Whittaker's style. "In many cases, the great things that are attributed to me or the institution have been what you might call children's crusades, and I say that with the very highest regard," he says.

He does hope that his students will be important avenues of commercialization. "So many are really going to change the world," he says. "They are the ones who will build great companies. The great ones depart academia." He proudly holds up a picture of himself with six students, two of whom have created a company called Velocity 11. They sold it to a larger company, Agilent. "So many of the great, great companies are not led by PhDs but by people who walked away" without earning degrees, Whittaker adds. This is one major avenue for ideas to emerge in Pittsburgh, and it is both a strength and a weakness. Graduate students are eager to create a company and then sell it within two or three years. They make a great deal of money and what they have done is a clear benefit to the larger corporations, but selling the company may result in economic activity being relocated elsewhere.

Other times, the economic activity stays and even expands after a big company buys a local company. McKesson, the big pharmaceutical distributor, bought Automated Health Care, a Pittsburgh start-up, and now employs hundreds in the Pittsburgh region. The bigger company possessed the distribution system to sell the smaller company's Robot RX across the country. This is an entire room that is built into a hospital. A scanner reads bar codes on prescriptions and then fills the orders, dropping them in a tray for pickup. It is both economical—because it can run seven days a week, twenty-four hours a day—and safer because it makes fewer mistakes than human operators might.

In a perfect world, the majority of companies that are born in the area would remain, grow into billion-dollar enterprises, and hire thousands of employees at high wages. But Whittaker does not fault his graduates for selling their companies; they certainly have a right to make money. After they do sell and their noncompete agreements expire, many of them will move on to the next idea.

Whittaker says he is committed to commercialization, which he calls "driving ideas into the world." He says he has been involved in the creation of twenty companies, either directly or through his students who took an idea and ran with it. But can a man like Whittaker be both a scientific genius and a commercial titan? And how can cutting-edge ideas from this idea factory be best diffused into the economy? Those questions dominate any debate about the future of Pittsburgh—and America.

Raj Rajkumar is younger than Whittaker and hails from the southern Indian state of Tamil Nadu, but he seems one step closer to deciding how work done inside the ivied halls of academe will percolate into the outside world.

Rajkumar, forty-six, is a professor of electrical and computer engineering and also the director of two research labs supported in part by General Motors. One is the Vehicular Information Technology lab and the other is the Autonomous Driving lab. GM's financial support for Whittaker's Urban Challenge was routed through Rajkumar's Autonomous Driving lab, so he was deeply involved in the project.

Whittaker's team built two vehicles using Chevy Tahoes—one was black and the other was tan—so that they would always have a backup vehicle in the event one developed technical problems or failed. They were both named "Boss," after Charles F. Kettering, a visionary research chief at General Motors. So, unofficially, the vehicles were called BossBlack and BossTan.

They were loaded with three kinds of expensive sensing devices—lasers, proximity radar (which was useful for adaptive cruise control), and cameras for night driving or driving in bad weather, when the other sensors would not be as effective. Together, these sensors captured images of what was happening on all sides of the vehicles.

Researchers put ten dual-core processors, or computers, inside each vehicle to process the large volumes of data coming from the sensors in real time, meaning instantaneously. The computers fused all the data into what was called a "coherent real-world model" of what was happening around the vehicle. This ability to knit together flows of information from different sensing devices is key to many of the robotic systems being made in Pittsburgh.

Then the researchers had to program the computers with the right algorithms, or rules of the road. When is it permissible to pass another vehicle on the road? What does the vehicle need to do if a child or bicycle suddenly darts out into the road? Based on what the algorithms dictated, the computers would then send the necessary signals to the steering wheel, gas pedal, or brakes.

When it came time for the 2007 competition, thirty-five different teams showed up to qualify on three different courses on a former air force base east of Los Angeles. The Carnegie Mellon team chose to enter BossTan in the race and had to be on the watch for many possible glitches. But this time they surmounted the technological obstacles and won. "It was one of the best experiences of my life," says Rajkumar. "It was technical, but it was a fascinating human event. We proved to the world that what they thought was science fiction could be accomplished in the short term."[3]

He can see how some of the knowledge gleaned from the Urban Challenge is finding its way into the private sector. GM already has deployed blind-spot monitors on some vehicles. The way those monitors work is that if a vehicle is behind you and on the side, in the spot where drivers cannot detect another vehicle, a sensor picks that up and sends a signal to a small light on the driver's side mirror. Other ideas under development at GM include adaptive cruise control, which would automatically apply the brakes and slow a vehicle down if it was approaching another vehicle too fast. Other "active safety features" could help keep a vehicle in a single lane on the highway. It's difficult to know whether GM developed these ideas on its own and merely confirmed their validity from the Urban Challenge or whether it incorporated them directly. But the parallels are unmistakable.

A bit further out on the horizon, Rajkumar has just demonstrated a concept called the Virtual Valet. It works this way: If a family went to a shopping mall, the car would drop them at the front door and go park itself. Then when the family was done shopping, they could summon the car to come pick them up at the front door. "Our ultimate goal is to have a vehicle drive itself," he says.

He says he can imagine a whole industry springing up in the Pittsburgh region to help make it happen. Cars equipped with autonomous driving would be able to take over on long stretches of interstate highway so that the driver does not get groggy. Stuck in a traffic jam at 5 mph? Turn over control to the vehicle and relax. The systems also would be useful for seniors who can't drive because they are too old, for busy people who want to catch up on e-mail, or for others who simply want to catch up on their sleep.

In this vision of the automotive future, each car would be connected to a wireless 3G network and communicate to other vehicles about traffic or slippery road conditions. They also could communicate with bridges and tunnels. Vehicles thus could find new routes around bad traffic or weather. Traffic fatalities would decline, and the amount of time Americans spend stuck in traffic also would decline. To make this happen, researchers and the industry would have to overcome legal and societal issues, to be sure; many drivers would resist allowing vehicles to take over the driving. And Rajkumar anticipates a burst of class action lawsuits if a single vehicle ever had an accident that caused damage or injuries.

But he insists this new industry can be born. "Over the next five to ten years, the technology will be there," he says.

Of course, it will take major support from industry, governments, and investors to create an autonomous driving cluster. "Why is Pittsburgh not the Silicon Valley of the East?" Rajkumar asks. "We're missing some ingredients. We have hundreds of start-up companies in different industries. But no Apple or Google. That part has not happened here yet. We'll keep pounding on the doors, and one of these days a door will open." One of the biggest missing pieces is the right sort of patient, intelligent venture capital.

Even if the vision of a new autonomous driving industry is still just a dream, none of it would be within reach without DARPA, says Rajkumar, and this relates to the national debate about industrial policy. DARPA's strategy is to fund researchers so that they can prove a concept, such as autonomous driving (which has huge military applications as well as civilian ones), and then move on to the next proof of concept. It assumes that once an idea has been demonstrated, the private sector will fund its commercialization. "I'm a strong believer in government having a proactive industrial policy," Rajkumar asserts. "This is how all the nations of Europe and Asia do it. The debate about having the government get out of the economy is the wrong debate."

He notes that military investments were key to making the Internet and GPS become realities. "The right investments can make a huge difference. How do these projects get funded and produce socially valuable results? Most of the funding comes from the government. It's a very small percentage of GNP, but the return value to the GNP is enormous."

Another idea that could transform the world comes from the feet of geckos, the lizards that Geico television commercials have made famous. This will be a key test of Carnegie Mellon's ability to let its ideas prosper in the outside world.

Metin Sitti, about forty, comes from an upper-middle-class family in Istanbul. He attended university in Istanbul and then went to the University of Tokyo for three years to earn a PhD.

That was a huge challenge because it required him to master the Japanese language. He also speaks English and German, and is now an associate professor in the NanoRobotics Laboratory, located within Carnegie Mellon's Robotics Institute.

Whereas Whittaker builds big robotic vehicles, Sitti builds nanorobots, as tiny as possible, some almost invisible. He wants these tiny robots to go into a volcano to determine if an eruption is imminent or to go into small passages within the human body for medical purposes. Lots of these little robots could be distributed in a body of water to sense pollution. In that case, they would be part of what he calls mobile sensor networks. To build these robots, Sitti has studied insects, such as the water strider, which travels over the surface of a pond. He also looks at small animals to see how they move and how they control themselves in complex environments.

Building nanorobots that could fly or swim was more difficult than making ones that could climb, so he concentrated on climbing. He attracted some funding from Boeing and NASA. They wanted sensor-equipped robots to climb inside planes' wings and fuselages for inspection and maintenance purposes.

As is often the case with scientific discoveries, serendipity played a key role in Sitti's breakthrough. How could robots climb walls? Wheels or treads would not work. But a biologist friend who had been to Thailand had grown fascinated with geckos, which can scamper up and down walls and across ceilings with ease.

Using high-powered microscopes, Sitti began examining gecko feet. He expected to find some sort of adhesive oils, but there were none. It turned out the feet possess a system of hairs only 5 microns in diameter, which then branch into smaller hairs and then into even smaller hairs, much like the branches of a tree. At the very end of these hair systems are tiny suction-like devices. So the gecko's feet easily adhere to different surfaces, including ones that are uneven. "The attachment force is huge," Sitti explains.[4]

Nine years ago, he was able to copy the gecko hair system, using nanofabrication templates in a clean-room environment. His patented gecko tape firmly adheres to a surface, like the best tape would, and it can't be yanked off. If you peel the sample by the edge, however, it comes off easily and doesn't leave any kind of sticky residue. So it's better than Scotch tape, which can leave a residue, and also better than Velcro, which requires two special surfaces.

The gecko adhesive could have big applications in sports gloves and sports clothing, assuming it would be approved by sports authorities. Imagine a football receiver racing toward the goal line with a pass from the quarterback hanging high above his shoulder. The receiver might be able to snag the ball with just a few fingers.

The military also sees big applications, which is why the air force and Department of Defense, together with the National Science Foundation (NSF), granted $500,000 in start-up financing for Sitti to start a company in 2009 called nanoGriptech, located two blocks from campus.

What's still not clear is whether Sitti knows what it takes to create a successful company. The key breakthrough occurred nine years ago, but it was only in 2009 that he started an actual company to exploit it commercially. The fact that he has now created a corporate headquarters two blocks off campus seems just a tiny step in what will most probably become a long journey.

The key to whether someone like Sitti is successful lies in the ecosystem that Carnegie Mellon and other institutions in Pittsburgh create. The starting point for encouraging ideas to flow out of Carnegie Mellon is the technology transfer office at the university, which was once a barrier, not an expediter. Entrepreneurs who attempted to take ideas from the university years ago tell stories about how the tech office insisted on controlling the upstarts no matter how many other investors they were able to attract. That was a very different approach from what MIT has taken. In recent years Carnegie Mellon's tech transfer office has changed its leadership, and today it has a much more enlightened policy. But its past policies may be one reason that more companies have not taken root and grown to substantial size in the area.

Outside the classroom, there are a variety of incubators and support organizations. An incubator is a physical facility where researchers can obtain space to develop their ideas into commercial products and where they may receive expert assistance. The National Robotics Engineering Consortium (NREC), located a few miles away along the Allegheny River, is part of Carnegie Mellon. It allows about fifty principal researchers to raise their own money for independent projects and hire students to work on them. There are also several key nonprofits. The Technology Collaborative, for example, obtains funding from state and federal governments and from local foundations, and gives grants to researchers to build their first prototypes. Other organizations get involved slightly later in the process and concentrate on loans, not grants. The Idea Foundry and Innovation Works are not-for-profit economic development organizations that seek to nurture an entrepreneur with seed-stage loans until the point that commercial investors are interested. They try to help entrepreneurs survive the valley of death, a period of years in which they must spend money to develop their ideas but are not able to reap commercial sales to fund that work.

Whereas Americans as a whole seem to understand the art of funding research inside a university, there is much less certainty about the next stage of developing the ideas. The scientists need to create alliances with business-minded executives, including those who understand marketing, finance, and distribution. One common formula is for the scientist to recruit a chief executive officer with experience, while becoming a chief scientist or chief technology officer, much as Chiang from MIT did at A123.

Another way is to play the role of matchmaker and try to find larger companies that want to strike up relationships with the producers of new ideas, which is what the Technology Collaborative does. "That is the right combination," says William A. Thomasmeyer, executive vice president of the Tech Collaborative and himself a serial entrepreneur for twenty-five years in information technology. "If you can pair a major corporation with an early-state or start-up company that's closely aligned with the university, that's the ticket for economic growth."[5]

The way the money flows to would-be entrepreneurs is key. The debate among CEOs in Pittsburgh is whether the NREC has too much of a nonprofit mentality. It encourages faculty and students to obtain federal funding for a project and then move on to the next grant. The incentives for them are not to "commercialize or perish." The reliance on federal grants may lead to a series of one-off experiments, rather than the mass manufacturing of hundreds or thousands of devices. And the grants given by foundations are widely distributed in small amounts. Instead, say some, they should be concentrated in larger quantities on the ideas that have the best chances and on the entrepreneurs who show the most progress in adopting commercial mind-sets. There must be a precise calibration of funding to create the right set of incentives for entrepreneurs. Too much of the wrong kind of funding makes them fat and happy. Too little starves them.

No matter what kind of ecosystem is in place, a final key is personality, and no one can control that variable. "For a lot of the scientists, one of the transitions they have to undergo is recognizing that creating a successful company is not only about the technology," Thomasmeyer of the Tech Collaborative says. "It's about engineering, production, support, and marketing. That's a learning curve for a lot of guys coming out of the university and trying to build companies." Some scientists find themselves bored by the mundane details of running a company and return to their labs; others find mechanisms to stay involved as scientific advisers. If he's lucky, Sitti could one day face that quandary.

Scott Friedman is one young Pittsburghian who navigated his way through the valley of death to create what is today a successful business. Friedman, forty-two, is chief executive officer of Seegrid Corp. and has just moved his company from Pittsburgh out into an industrial park west of town, past the airport. The reason for the move is that his company, which is still privately held, has just expanded from twenty to forty people. It makes 1,400-pound robots that can transport loads of 8,000 pounds in warehouses.

Friedman graduated from high school in 1985, a time when many young people wanted to leave Pittsburgh. "Everybody who could fog a mirror and didn't have a family business was getting out of town," he says.[6]

Like his friends, he went away to school, graduating from the University of Michigan, then earning a medical degree from the University of West Virginia. Along the way, he created a medical-related software company and sold it to Philips, the Dutch electronics giant. That helped him start amassing capital.

Back home at last, he partnered with a director of the Mobile Robotics Lab at Carnegie Mellon's Robotics Institute, and found an angel investor, an emergency room physician. Friedman's ability to raise money for Seegrid is all the more remarkable because investors have lost hundreds of millions of dollars investing in robots since the 1980s. "All the money got flushed away and nothing worked," he explains.

The reason is that making advanced robotic systems is more challenging than making a robot that performs repetitive tasks in an auto factory, which is mere closed-loop automation. Like Whittaker, he's derisive about robots that simply do the same thing over and over. "The real world is sloppier and less rational," he says. The problem is that there may be 250 forklift operators in a big distribution center or warehouse, so any robotic vehicle moving goods has to be much more sensitive and interactive. "The level of complexity is so extreme that they need a different way of thinking about how to help the operators," he says. In such a setting, there is constant interaction between people and their robotic helpers. People can tap commands into laptop computers that control the robot vehicles.

Part of Friedman's success seems to be that he has made the key psychological transition—he's fascinated with devising a business model that works, seemingly more than he is fascinated with the underlying technology. The robots have two "eyes" that allow them to create grids on what they see ahead of them, hence the name of the company. Seegrid concentrates only on the software, and buys all the other components standard off the shelf. The robots themselves come from a Japanese supplier. The DVD screens on the robots are similar to what are on sale at Walmart. A committed technologist might insist on building the robot from scratch with state-of-the-art gear, but Friedman has worked out how to make them and sell them for just $65,000. "We've figured out a price point," he explains.

But he also got lucky, technologically speaking. CMOS sensors, or cameras, that serve as the eyes used to cost him $380 apiece but are now only $45. Intel semiconductor chips used in the laptops as the brains of the robots are three times as fast as they were when he started. The laptops now have much larger memory drives and can therefore hold 30 miles of robot pathways. For the past twenty-five years, mobile robotics has been in the impossible stage. Now rapid advances in the underlying technologies are changing that equation. "Most of these robotic problems are going to be trivial within ten years," he predicts.

Didn't he make huge bets on things he couldn't control? "You have to," he explains, with wisdom beyond his years. "Otherwise you're road kill."

But the most important thing Friedman did was to face the market and seek to discover what it wanted, and at what price. He did not remain fascinated by the technology alone.

The classic Pittsburgh case that demonstrates the difficulty—and rewards—of commercializing a technology is RedZone Robotics, founded by Whittaker in 1987. It was his commercialization arm, and it made a series of robots including the clean-up vehicles for the Chernobyl meltdown and robots that would inspect sewer lines. They were mostly one-off, specialized pieces of equipments, rather than standardized products sold on a larger scale.

In the late 1990s, Whittaker met Eric Close, who was a different kind of student because he wasn't in engineering or robots, but rather was at Carnegie's business school, studying to get an MBA. Whittaker tried to lure Close to RedZone in 2000, but the young man demurred. He had developed a fascination for turning around bankrupt companies, and moved to the Philadelphia area to do just that—buying and turning around a series of three companies in the fields of construction equipment parts, rail car manufacturing, and software. He was a serial turnaround expert.

Whittaker's path crossed his again in 2002 when RedZone finally went bankrupt. Whittaker could not truly make the company grow into profitability. So he called Close, who was just finishing the third turnaround. This time Whittaker was able to persuade him, and Close took over the company in September 2002.

The company remained in bankruptcy while Close tried to figure out what product it could make on a commercial scale. He dug into the details of all the different robotic devices that RedZone had built to find one that was "scalable." To make money, a company has to identify a product and make a lot of it—in different variations perhaps, but it has to achieve scale. "Commercialization is hard," says Close, who is today forty. "It works when you are market-driven, not technology-driven."[7]

The answers started becoming clearer for Close when the city of Pittsburgh was being sued by the U.S. Environmental Protection Agency because its local sewer systems were overflowing during storms, sixty to eighty days a year, into the Allegheny and Monongahela rivers, which join to form the Ohio River.

Close realized that there were all sorts of problems with the infrastructure of water and sewage lines beneath cities around the country and around the world. Aside from sewage spills during storms, tree roots may grow in the pipes, blocking them. Pipes may shift physical position slightly, creating fissures; oils and greases from restaurants also can create difficulties. The vast majority of cities don't know what's underground, much less what kind of condition the systems are in—much of the infrastructure, at least in the United States, is fifty to seventy years old. "People don't know where the pipes are," he explains. "No one documented it." It was a huge untapped market.

So he decided to concentrate on robots that would enter sewer and water lines. The company came out of bankruptcy in June 2003. Its 20-pound robots, made in Ohio, are either battery-powered or electric-powered. They are inserted into a sewer or water system through manholes and go through the pipes to the next manhole, and so on. They are equipped with lasers, sonar, distance sensors, tilt sensors, and similar devices. They have zoom vision to concentrate on a particular spot and also have fish-eye vision to obtain a complete image of the inside of a pipe. They carry a gas monitor to detect certain kinds of gases.

The robot collects all the relevant information about the system, and when it comes back up, it provides the data to the company's analysis department. RedZone then creates a computerized model of the system, which it shares with the customer. What Google Earth does for mapping surface objects, "we do for all the underground infrastructure," Close explains. Municipalities can use the robots to inspect their systems on a regular basis in an effort to catch problems before they erupt and require tens of millions of dollars to fix under emergency conditions.

With the key technological challenges behind him, Close is concentrating on the "productization" of the robots. "You have to have management that can take these disruptive forces in the markets and actually commercialize them," he says. That requires managing people with many different skills—electrical engineering, mechanical engineering, civil engineering, software, manufacturing, field deployment and field services, analysis, and both direct and indirect sales channels. "It's like running GM," he jokes.

Today RedZone has $10 million in annual sales and sixty-five employees, and it sells its services in ninety cities in the United States, plus Hong Kong, Singapore, Malaysia, and Canada. "We should be a billion-dollar business at some point," Close says. That's the key threshold that has so far eluded Pittsburgh.

There's no doubt that the American engine of ideas is alive in Pittsburgh. It is attracting the best minds from around the world, from southern India to cosmopolitan Istanbul, and putting them in an environment where they can take risks and think outside the sometimes confining boundaries they faced at home. The flow of ideas is absolutely world-class, on par with MIT, Stanford, or any other top research institution.

The region's ecosystem for commercializing these ideas is not perfect, but it shows clear promise. One lesson is that people like Red Whittaker should concentrate on the frontiers of knowledge and not try to become CEOs. It is up to others to concentrate on the ecosystem that helps ideas emerge from Carnegie Mellon. Business managers must concentrate on nontechnological challenges—that is, expanding businesses—and this means attracting more people with the skills that Friedman and Close possess. The ideas must be passed down a chain of different personalities and skills before they can truly blossom.

Even though Pittsburgh is an older city, its systems and networks for putting "idea people" in touch with "business people" and "money people" are still relatively young. More established clusters such as Boston, Silicon Valley, and Austin have now enjoyed several generations of entrepreneurship and growth. Partly as a result of this gap, Pittsburgh's robotic entrepreneurs are not yet getting all the capital they need and all the experience and mentoring that comes with smart money. But if Pittsburgh can persevere to create an advanced robotics industry, perhaps including a cluster of autonomous driving companies, it will establish that even cities perceived as being in the Rust Belt can successfully transform themselves and create wealth for future generations. Decline is not inevitable. Renewal is distinctly possible.

THREE

★ ★ ★

How the Military Innovates
Orlando's Simulation Boom

MANSOOREH MOLLAGHASEMI GREW UP in an upper-middle-class family in Tehran. An avid student, she took summer classes and excelled in math and science, allowing her to skip from the Iranian version of the fourth grade to the seventh.

But Ayatollah Khomeini and other religious figures were on the verge of toppling Shah Mohammad Reza Pahlavi, the country's autocratic ruler. Anticipating a period of convulsive change, the family sent Mansooreh and her brothers to the United States for their college educations. In 1978, she went to the University of Louisville in Kentucky without speaking English. "My brothers and I came out to get an education and never went back," she says now. The mullahs, who took charge in 1979, "would not have let us advance. They didn't want intellectuals."[1]

In this case, Iran's loss was America's gain. Mollaghasemi earned a PhD in industrial engineering at the University of Louisville and in 1991 migrated to Orlando, where she became part of that city's aspirations to create a cluster based on computer simulation and modeling. At forty-nine, she is the chief executive officer of Productivity Apex, which has more than twenty employees and has cracked the $3 million level in annual sales. She's also a tenured professor at the University of Central Florida (UCF), where she teaches classes on simulation.

The origins of Orlando's simulation cluster lie in the decisions by the U.S. military and major defense contractors in the 1950s to locate major operations in or near Orlando, by NASA to locate the Kennedy Space Center about an hour away, and by Disney and Universal to locate entertainment parks on the western side of town beginning in the 1960s. More than a hundred companies are engaged in simulation work, ranging from defense giants such as Lockheed Martin and Science Applications International Corp. (SAIC) down to companies such as Mollaghasemi's.

Computer gaming is another major element of the creative stew because Electronic Arts' Tiburon Studio develops many of its sports games in Orlando. Military simulation, entertainment, and gaming have thus converged, and UCF, scarcely known on the national stage, has become an idea factory, churning out both technologies and students to work for these companies.

Orlando is no utopia. The small city exploded into a metropolitan area with 2.2 million people, resulting in much of Orlando feeling very new and crassly commercial. During the bubble years, hundreds of thousands of people moved into the area, which meant that real estate values kept rising and the construction industry was busy. Hordes of tourists flocked to the entertainment parks. Seemingly endless commercial strips and malls did big business.

Now those aspects of Orlando's economy are struggling because of recession and the end of easy credit. Squeezed by tougher credit card conditions among other factors, tourists are cutting back on their visits to Disney and Universal, and shuttered stores are not an uncommon sight. Florida as a whole has suffered its first net population outflow, as people continue to move elsewhere to find work. For these reasons, Orlando's effort to create a knowledge-based economy is all the more important because these jobs should be more resistant to the ups and downs of the economy.

Orlando, far from being a sleepy southern tourist town, has attracted people of all stripes and nationalities. Mollaghasemi, as one example, earned her PhD with a dissertation on "multi-criteria optimization of simulation models."

To understand that, think back to the scientific method that was taught in high school chemistry class. If you had four variables in an experiment, you would try to keep three of those variables constant while changing the fourth to see what would happen. Then you could prove that changing the fourth variable in a certain way was the right way to produce a certain result.

But the real world isn't that simple. More than one variable might change at the same time, meaning several conflicting measures of performance must be simultaneously considered. There is also a degree of randomness and uncertainty. Not everything happens according to a rational formula. Analytical methods may be scientific, but they are not fast and robust enough to handle rapidly changing, complex issues. So a model that can simulate what happens in real-world conditions is obviously very valuable in the world of business. That's what Mollaghasemi is a genius at figuring out. She creates simulation models that mimic what happens in reality.

She was so good at this field that after she made a presentation at a conference in Orlando in 1991, the chairman of UCF's Industrial Engineering Department offered her a job, and she moved to Florida.

Mollaghasemi has taught there ever since but has never been completely content in the confines of academia. She always wanted exposure to real-world problems; during a couple of summers, she worked at AT&T Microelectronics, which was a huge fabrication facility for semiconductors until it was closed. But even that was not enough.

So she created her company in 2001 and started explaining her skills at workshops to find customers—and she hit it big at the very first one, held at NASA. "A gentleman who was in the audience came up to me and said they had just done a strategic plan for NASA and simulation had come out as one of the top technologies for improving NASA's processes," Mollaghasemi recalls. "They wanted to see if I could model the entire shuttle hardware processing, to see how the shuttle comes together in a timely manner, because you have a launch window that you have to meet. That's how I got started."

NASA wanted help in understanding where bottlenecks might be occurring in its supply chain, say, that delayed its ability to examine all the parts of a landed shuttle, then reassemble it and relaunch it. They wanted to speed up the process and so, improbably, turned to a refugee from Iran to help. "At first I didn't have a clue what NASA was talking about," Mollaghasemi explains. "I had meetings with the technical officer from NASA every Tuesday for four hours to go through a particular process. That's how I learned their language." She also was able to win a high security clearance.

For the shuttle relaunch, Mollaghasemi and her team at Productivity Apex devised a "process map," a step she performs for all her clients. These maps can take up an entire wall in a conference room or office. Then she transfers that knowledge into statistical modeling programs on computers that attempt to replicate real-world conditions.

She explains NASA's process: "The shuttle lands. It goes to an orbiter processing facility. They take things apart. Each step requires a process. Then after they check it, they put it back together. It goes to the vehicle assembly building. They stack the solid rocket boosters, they put on the external tanks, and finally the orbiter is attached. Then it rolls out to the pad. All these processes are variable—one time it takes ten days, the next time it may take twenty days, depending on what problems you find. Because of that randomness and because you're looking at dynamic behavior in the system, no pencil and paper, and no fancy analysis, can capture this. The only way is through simulation."

At first she located her corporate headquarters in a hole-in-the-wall office on University Boulevard near UCF, but she did not truly know anything about creating a business. She clearly needed help. So in 2003, she moved her offices to UCF's incubator, which happens to be one of the nation's best. "Mansooreh was good at simulation; she wasn't so good at running a company," says Tom O'Neal, associate vice president for research and commercialization in charge of the incubator. "She knew how to answer questions like 'What is a variance?' or 'What is a standard deviation?' but we had to translate the technology into a business opportunity."[2]

That meant answering questions such as: How would she manage a company? How would she hire additional people? What is cash flow and how would she manage that? O'Neal helped her hire a chief operating officer and chief financial officer, even sitting in on some interviews. He also exposed her to mentoring by introducing her to other CEOs of comparably sized companies who were trying to grow and survive. She did not choose to raise capital, partly because Orlando has a shortage of venture capitalists but also because she did not want to borrow money, preferring to fund her company with existing contracts. "If she borrowed, she could grow quicker," O'Neal explains. "But she doesn't want to."

While she was getting up to speed on how to run a company, Mollaghasemi's business kept expanding. A new customer was Orlando International Airport, which has been a busy one for years because of all the tourists descending on the city's entertainment facilities. She created a model of the entire airport, taking into consideration traffic conditions outside the airport, delays at the curb where passengers are dropped off, ticketing, security, and the departure gate. "We're modeling the airport on our computers," she explains, "so that if they want to move gates around, they don't have to go physically tell Delta 'You move here' and tell Virgin 'You move here' and then observe it for a few days to see what happens." That would be the old-fashioned way of experimenting.

Instead, "we capture the 'as is,' as we call it, on the computer, and once we validate it, we start playing what-if games. What if we combine Southwest and Delta in one wing? What is the impact on the security checkpoint? What if Southwest does away with all their ticketing agents and installs just e-ticketing

Shumaker, sixty-four, was once director of the navy's artificial intelligence lab, then worked at the Naval Research Laboratory. Ninety percent of his institute's budget is from research contracts and grants, ranging from Lockheed Martin, which is trying to create decision-training systems, to small civilian companies such as Chi Systems, based in Pennsylvania, which sells lifelike medical training systems. Some 60 percent of his funding is defense-related, the other 40 percent civilian.

One of Shumaker's pet subjects is biomorphic computing, which has to do with how humans use technology. "We're already pre-tuned to incorporate technology," he says. "We have absolutely no problem using a telephone or a computer or a hammer or driving a car or flying an aircraft. When we do those things, we don't think about the details. We learn to make it part of our bodies. Fighter pilots talk about strapping on the airplane, rather than getting into the airplane. What they mean is, they get in and they cease to be separate. They think about doing something and it happens. So why not take advantage of our natural tendencies to that?"[4]

That is clearly related to simulation and has obvious military implications, but what can simulation offer to other industries? "Every field has the need for or already has simulation systems— that is, creating models and making complicated things usable," he explains. Pilots already learn how to fly on simulators, and teenagers may take driving lessons on simulators. Weathermen also use simulation to take existing wind conditions or rain patterns and project them forward for twenty-four or forty-eight hours.

But consider the possibilities in the worlds of psychology and medicine. Shumaker's institute has conducted one experiment that used simulation to help a patient who had a stroke and lost his ability to make decisions. Shumaker says the patient's "executive ability," or the ability to decide what to do first and what to do second, was impaired. He had been undergoing regular therapy for six months but had made limited progress. It still took him two hours in the morning to make a breakfast consisting of coffee, cereal, and a bagel. He couldn't remember where anything was stored, not spoons, not sugar, not anything.

So researchers created a virtual world for the patient, a safe space, to make the therapy more effective. Near Shumaker's office is a theater where they did the work. It's an empty room with just a blue screen in the backdrop. The researchers used stage sets, cheap kitchen cabinets, a real refrigerator, and a real coffeemaker to create a computer program that bore a remarkable resemblance to the man's own kitchen. To orient him, the researchers even made it appear that it could look into his own living room. People with experience in the theater and entertainment fields helped create the program.

It seemed to work. "His therapist said he made more progress in six weeks than the previous six months," Shumaker explains. "Somehow his brain was getting rewired." The patient was able to dramatically reduce the number of footsteps he used to search the kitchen and also to cut the amount of time it took to prepare breakfast.

Shumaker sees the possibility of working with other patients who have phobias or impairments, such as stuttering in public places. In an experiment to help stutterers, researchers have created a virtual restaurant with eighteen other tables. The noise and bustle can be dialed up gradually to help desensitize a stutterer to the background noises. Working with a human therapist, the patient can practice and improve in a safe environment.

Shumaker also foresees a multibillion-dollar medical simulation industry. In a studio, he displays a lifelike artificial arm that generates a pulse. It is a training device for military medics to learn how to apply a tourniquet. "Getting a lecture on how to apply a tourniquet isn't like actually doing it," he says. That device could be very helpful to ambulance workers and nurses across the country.

He then displays a model of an upper body that has taken a grievous injury to the face—teeth have been knocked out and lips ripped off. There is a gaping, bloody hole where there used to be a mouth. The goal of this simulation is to figure how to keep the airways open and avoid a collapsed lung. When is it time to insert an artificial breathing device through the throat so that the patient doesn't drown in his or her own blood? This also was developed for the military, but it could be used in medical schools around the world.

In the realm of educational simulation, Shumaker's researchers created a virtual classroom with UCF's College of Education, which Lockheed Martin is now trying to sell to school districts. The goal is to help new teachers learn how to manage the complex dynamics of the classroom. The would-be teachers face a computer screen that has six or eight students, or avatars, displayed on it. They are cartoonish in physical appearance, but real-life actors, located elsewhere, control the students' facial movements and behavior, not to mention the words they utter. One student is the class bully, another is painfully withdrawn. Still another is bright and eager. The teacher can watch the interactions among the students and can approach a single student, whose face then fills up the screen. The actors, in this case called "interactors," are highly skilled. The goal is to help the student teacher learn how to control a classroom and reach the kids who want to learn.

The availability of artists, cartoonists, set designers, and actors is key to building these virtual worlds. The entertainment industry knows how to do that. "They know how to build believable scenarios," Shumaker says. "Typically, a company might have great technology and they try to create realistic uses for that. But their technical people might not understand how people like to interact with their product. But we have those people who can do it."

Shumaker tries to create a crossroads effect at his institute by seeking sustained interactions among the people who understand different technologies and disciplines. That involves working with professors and experts in psychology, engineering, computer science, math, physics, and education, all of whom are conveniently located within walking distance. "The interfaces between fields are where interesting things are happening," Shumaker adds.

He believes that, increasingly, America's basic research will be done in places such as his institute. Companies are focusing their research and development efforts on applied research, or the development end of the R&D world, which essentially means working with existing knowledge to get products into the market. He notes that Bell Labs is gone. "The era of the great industrial research labs is over, so where does the stuff get done? We are claiming we can be your company's research lab."

This is a bold statement. He's offering innovation on demand, in effect. Innovation does not have to occur by accident, even though that's the traditional view of how a technology spins off from the military. Shumaker wants to create the commercial use at about the same time that the military is perfecting a technology, what he calls a secondary spin-off. "We want to grow technology that may be too expensive or too complicated for civilian use and then scale it down," he says.

At sixty-four, Shumaker says he isn't about to retire. He gives off the air of a man who has a lot left to accomplish.

If Shumaker is the foreman of the idea factory, then M. J. Soileau is the idea salesman. Head of UCF's commercialization efforts, Soileau carries the nickname "Ragin' Cajun" because he is from southwest Louisiana, born on the banks of the Yellow Bayou, the ninth generation of French-speakers to live there.

But the young Cajun had to get out of Louisiana to build the career he wanted. He earned a doctorate from the University of Southern California in electrical engineering and quantum electronics in 1979 and spent a year near Boston's Route 128 working in the earliest stages of the still unproven personal computer industry.

Soileau, now about sixty, with a gray beard and glasses, has thought deeply about the creation of wealth and his own role in it. "What we're trying to do here is different than just the redistribution of wealth, which is to a certain extent what service industries do," he says.[5] This is controversial to some Americans, who argue that the service sector—meaning banking, consulting, retailing, and similar industries—can sustain the U.S. economy even in the absence of manufacturing.

Soileau doesn't buy it. "It's got to be something other than borrowing money to buy Chinese-manufactured goods at Walmart," he continues. "I'm not an economist by training, but even to a geek like me, that doesn't seem like it's sustainable in the long run. So somebody has to create wealth. You can pump wealth out of the ground, but if you can't pump it out of the ground, you have to create it. What we are concentrating on here is knowledge-based wealth, that is, wealth produced from intellectual property. It starts with having key people who create that intellectual property." Those ideas come from Shumaker and fellow researchers.

This is where Soileau's commercialization efforts come in. "You need to put the same amount of creativity and energy into the commercialization of that intellectual property as you did to create it in the first place," he explains. "You need the same conscious, focused effort, with a different group of people, perhaps."

In short, the brightest researchers may come up with brilliant ideas, but they lack the skills to commercialize those ideas, and in many cases they're not even interested in doing that. People with knowledge of marketing and financing, for example, have to be the ones who take the ideas and run with them.

One piece of what Soileau does is oversee the incubator, which Tom O'Neal manages on a day-to-day basis. The UCF incubator now has eighty companies in it, and more than a hundred have gone through it. Of those, thirty-four "graduated," meaning they created successful companies. Thirty-one of those thirty-four stayed in Orlando, including Mollaghasemi's. As a result, the incubator has created more than 1,650 jobs and $200 million in local economic impact, according to a recent study. Most of the companies are still small. "We can't say we have a Hewlett-Packard yet,"

Soileau acknowledges. "It's been a story of starting by the boot-straps and yanking real hard and pulling yourself up. We don't have venture capital, so what do we do about it? We get venture money from outside the area." The incubator also taps the Small Business Administration for start-up cash. Altogether it has raised $190 million over ten years.

The companies being nurtured include those from a variety of fields, not just simulation. Cognoscenti Health Institute, which picks up medical samples and performs high-end diagnostics overnight, is one of them. Another is Rini Technologies, which licensed laser technology from UCF. The original technology was aimed at cooling lasers when they get too hot. But Dan Rini, founder of the firm bearing his name, is working on using that know-how to create ultraportable, handheld air conditioners for soldiers serving in 100-degree-plus heat in Iraq or Afghanistan. "That's a pretty typical pattern in technology," Soileau explains. "You develop it to solve one problem and it proves to be more useful for other things."

Aside from helping Mollaghasemi, the incubator has helped Russians and people of other nationalities who barely understand capitalism. "Only in America," Soileau says. "You'll find very few countries that give immigrants the same kind of opportunities at the highest levels of education as we do." This is a recurring theme—to create wealth, a region needs to attract the smartest people from a variety of cultures.

As at MIT and Carnegie Mellon, how a university manages intellectual property is a huge subject, and Soileau is right in the thick of that issue. "Intellectual property comes in all forms," he explains. "You can't own somebody else's know-how. You can't patent it or copyright it."

In some cases, UCF wants to help a professor create wealth by helping him or her through the incubator, but it doesn't make any claim to the underlying know-how. In other cases, the university licenses technology developed there and demands a piece of the action, but not so much that it discourages commercial-

ization. In others, it does research under contract with a corporation or government entity, which is Shumaker's specialty.

The guiding philosophy is to use all the ideas, wherever they
come from, to create wealth in the Orlando area, not to hoard
the knowledge, as some universities are tempted to do by trying to maintain ironclad control over their intellectual property.
Soileau's ultimate goal is to adopt the best practices from the more
mature research universities. They are fueling their respective
clusters with ideas, and they have alumni who donate heavily
to them and offer jobs to graduates. "They are surrounded by a
rich ecosystem that they helped develop," he says. "We're trying
to build that ecosystem."

In the best ecosystems, there have to be the right kinds of interactions among researchers, and then different sets of people who
try to create companies or license the technology. There needs to
be a system of mentoring would-be CEOs and a supply of capital.
Others have done it; now Soileau hopes it is Orlando's turn. "In
a global economy, you're not going to have a high living standard
just by doing things cheaper than everybody else in the world," he
says. "It has to be based on knowledge and innovation."

Of course, not every start-up emerges from a university. Some
emerge because bright people choose to leave big companies.
They may locate in a specific place. Or else they take off because
they are poised at the intersection of two industries, a different
kind of crossroads effect. Bob Allen's company reflects all those
factors.

Allen was raised in Orange County, California. He joined Walt
Disney in California more than thirty years ago but begged to
be transferred out of what he regarded as a hopelessly congested,
urbanized part of the country to the relatively serene life of
Orlando. Whereas Mollaghasemi now works on the east side
of town, where most business is connected with the military
or NASA, Allen comes from the west side of Orlando, where

Disney and other big entertainment complexes are located. Allen worked in a postproduction studio for Disney for twenty-five years, mostly in Orlando, until 2001, when the company decided to sell the division, called Disney Production Services. He was able to put together enough money to buy it. How? "I did it the old-fashioned American way," he jokes. "I mortgaged my house and pretty much everything else I had."[6]

Today those operations are grouped together in a company called IDEAS. It's highly symbolic that Allen, now fifty-five, has recently moved his company to downtown Orlando, to a former television production studio owned by the *Orlando Sentinel*. The new location represents the convergence of East Coast and West Coast, of the military- and government-related world with the entertainment world.

Allen's business card identifies him as the "principal executive and chief storytelling officer" of the company, not the chief executive officer. The company averages about $5 million a year in sales of e-learning and simulation products, and employs twenty-five people full-time.

It's tricky to define just what IDEAS does. At Disney, Allen did postproduction work, which means all the things that occur after a television show has been shot on a set. That includes special effects, fixing color or sound, and editing of all sorts. It was a little unusual to be located three thousand miles from headquarters in southern California, but "we were okay," he recalls. "We were having a good time."

The digital revolution, combined with Disney's reevaluation of its business structure, changed everything and opened new creative doors. Allen recalls: "We said to ourselves, 'Let's tack on creative capacity in front of what we were doing. And why stick with TV? Let's take an idea from conception all the way through to completion. Why not become a full-blown studio?' " That line of thinking created what Allen calls an "innovation studio"—part television production agency, part advertising agency, part simulation company.

The biggest single piece of IDEAS' business has been Battlestations 21, a gripping, immersive simulation program for the U.S. Navy. It started because the navy realized it needed to do a better job training fifty thousand recruits a year in how to actually function in combat situations. This age group grew up playing video games, so the navy began talking to Allen about how to create, in effect, the mother of all video games to train them. "It took three meetings to create a glossary of terms so that the two sides could understand each other," Allen recalls. The air was thick with acronyms. But the navy knew what it wanted. "They said, 'We want you guys to take these eight scenarios and 147 learning objectives and package them,'" Allen explains. "So we did." His company was the prime contractor and worked with several other companies to complete the project.

The fourteen-hour program is quite literally immersive. It occurs in a 450-foot missile frigate in an indoor controlled environment inside the Great Lakes Recruit Training Center, north of Chicago. Explosions erupt. Water pours in. Horns and sirens erupt, and red lights blink overhead. Actors playing the role of officers shout at the trainees, "Your ship is burning and you are wasting time." It's the very picture of chaos, and it isn't just on a computer screen. It surrounds the recruit through an entire night. "It will burn your eyebrows off," quips Allen.

Mannequins equipped with sound effects, who appear to be wounded comrades, are so realistic that when the human sailors are instructed to evacuate the wounded, they find themselves reassuring the dummies, "You're going to be okay. We're going to take care of you."

So why would the navy, or any civilian company, turn to an entertainment start-up for this kind of training assistance? It's because the entertainment industry knows how to get people to "suspend disbelief," as Allen explains. "There's a relationship that entertainers know about between you and an audience that isn't like any other relationship. It's very sacred. If you don't get the audience to fall in love with you, at least for the duration of the performance, you will fail. It's no different with a sailor. We need them to fall in love and join us in that story." The navy by itself can't do as good a job at that; nor can the vast majority of government entities or civilian enterprises.

In a civilian extension of its work, IDEAS creates content for the Florida Department of Emergency Management to help train the state's children how to respond to hurricanes and such. They've created a collection of children's stories and audiobooks that help kids learn how to read and at the same time teach them what they need to know about Florida's sometimes nasty weather. "They won't be afraid, but they'll know what to do in terms of emergency preparedness," Allen explains. "They'll know what an evacuation is all about."

In the health care sector, the company is working on training videos for nurses to help them learn how to use very sophisticated hospital beds. "We've got twenty-two minutes for an overworked, stressed nurse to try to learn how to use a new bed, a therapeutic device," Allen says. "If you use them right, you can save a life. But if you use them wrong, you can kill."

Education is another opportunity, but with a twist. Here the company is working on a product it calls Teacher Studio, which is a combination of YouTube and Facebook for educators in a safe, controlled environment. It's a professional network rather than an open social network. Teachers can upload their best practices, and other school districts can subscribe to the body of knowledge—at a price, of course. "This environment allows teachers for the first time to upload best practices," Allen explains. "If I've got a great way to teach DNA to seventh graders, I can take my phone and videotape what I do in my class. Then I marry that with a standard template for lesson planning. So if someone in Oshkosh needs a better way to teach DNA, he or she can pull up your lesson plan."

The connective tissue in all that IDEAS does, then, seems to be building communities in which people can collaborate. Those can be as fully immersive as Battlestations 21 or as minimal as a pair of headphones and a laptop for a child.

One key to Orlando's creativity, Allen argues, is the flow of talent into Disney, Universal, and Sea World—and then back out. People may leave those jobs, but at least some choose to stay in Orlando, creating a base of talented job seekers including many kinds of actors. "The thing I've learned how to do real well is take care of creative people and offer environments in which creative people can thrive," Allen says. "It isn't just twenty-year-olds on Razor scooters with earrings. That's a total cliché. The creative act is a natural, normal, and almost requisite part of a human being, and everybody's got it. So we don't have a creative department. That's not how we work. We're a new kind of company." Everyone is supposed to be creative, not just a handful of people.

Allen is a fan of the books of Richard Florida, who argues that knowledge workers are key to any city or nation's economic aspirations.[7] Which brings us back to Orlando. "It's a clean environment, it's safe," Allen says. "There are economic advantages. So I think the number one reason people come here is that it's a great place to live, which for the knowledge-worker group, or the creative group, is important."

IDEAS has not attracted any outside investors yet, but Allen wants it to grow to $60 million to $70 million in sales within a relatively short time. In January 2009 he recruited a CEO with twenty-five years of experience at IBM, who is very knowledgeable about the world of finance. It will fall to the new CEO to raise capital, while Allen concentrates on what he loves best—storytelling.

He could be speaking about himself when he returns to the theme of Richard Florida's creative class. "Pure creatives are less motivated by pure money than they are by how they feel about their lives," Allen argues. "If they feel good about where they live and can find common cause with people they find engaging, that's key." How do you manage such people? "That's the number one thing you have to do," he replies. "You can't let people get bored. Boredom is death. If you don't have enough work for them, you have to create something."

The lesson seems to be this: Follow the creative talent around the United States and the world. A place where talented professionals can find stimulation and satisfaction, and where they can be comfortable in terms of living standard and lifestyle, is where you most often find economic growth.

Obviously, many of the companies that have been created in Orlando are still small. For its simulation industry to grow and create statistically meaningful numbers of jobs, companies such as Productivity Apex and IDEAS need to grow more rapidly. The relative absence of angel investors and venture capitalists is a weakness in the Orlando ecosystem. For now, larger companies headquartered elsewhere—Lockheed Martin, SAIC, Electronic Arts, Disney—are the dominant players. Moreover, it's not yet clear that the wealth and jobs generated by this new simulation industry will compensate for losses in tourism, real estate, construction, and retailing.

But Orlando does offer a creative stew that is most promising if it can be guided in the right direction. Not only is it showing the way to the rest of Florida and to other Sunbelt states that bet the ranch on easy credit, but the simulation industry could also have a broad ripple effect on the American economy in sectors such as medicine, education, and logistics. The productivity gains could be enormous—and spending by the U.S. military and NASA will have played a major role in making it happen.

FOUR

Best and Brightest

San Diego's Genomics Industry Attracts
World-Class Talent

IVOR ROYSTON'S FATHER was born in Poland and his mother in Czechoslovakia. They met in England during World War II, got married, and had a family. They arrived in the United States in 1954, when Royston was nine years old.

Early on, it became clear that Royston was particularly driven and entrepreneurial. At age fourteen he declared that he would devote his life to curing cancer, well before President Nixon would later declare war on cancer. It wasn't because someone in his family had died of it—he was simply fascinated by a disease that was so deadly yet so poorly understood.

He went to medical school and became a cancer specialist, or oncologist, at the University of California at San Diego (UCSD). Rather than pursuing purely academic research, however, he became more interested in taking ideas out of the laboratory and using them in day-to-day medical work. In the 1970s, the two worlds of science and medicine remained apart, as scientists pursued knowledge but didn't push it into the medical world. Doctors, meanwhile, tended not to share details about patients and their conditions with the scientific community. Bridging this gap was called *translational* work (and still is).

After he developed monoclonal antibodies to help diagnose and treat cancer, Royston, as a lowly assistant professor, tried to get the university to help translate his knowledge into medical clinics. But the university was simply not equipped to do it. Many colleagues resented Royston for even trying to push his discovery into the marketplace. "It was heresy," he recalls. "There used to be secret meetings held by the faculty to try to decide what to do about me. I had a whole bunch of arrows shot at me. They said, 'How can you be a professor and start a company?' "[1] Professors from the engineering school at Stanford University had created Hewlett-Packard, but that was in another city and in another field. The concept was new to San Diego. Nor were large pharmaceutical companies interested in Royston's work.

He turned to Kleiner Perkins Caufield & Byers, one of the early dominant venture capital firms in Silicon Valley, which had funded Genentech, a pioneer in biotechnology in the San Francisco Bay Area. "The only way to move the antibodies into the clinic was to develop my own company, my own industry," says Royston. "It wasn't because I wanted to make money. I didn't even think about that. It was because I wanted to get these antibodies into patients."

Kleiner Perkins invested the princely sum of $300,000, and San Diego's first biotechnology company, Hybritech, was born in 1978. Royston and his associates went on to form or invest in dozens of other biotechs. Over time, Royston shifted roles and became a venture capitalist rather than a scientist or a doctor. He created Forward Ventures in 1993, and today it has $500 million under management and has bankrolled fifty companies with names such as Acorda Therapeutics, Dynavax, Epix Pharmaceuticals, Hypnion, and Morphotek. There are a total of six hundred life sciences companies in San Diego and its tony suburb of La Jolla, including diagnostic and device firms. That means Royston and his Forward Ventures helped create a hefty percentage of the companies in the biotech cluster, which is on par with those in the San Francisco Bay Area and the Boston region in terms of total employment and number of companies.

In doing all this, Royston helped transform a sleepy town

once known for its U.S. Navy base, the San Diego Zoo, the savings and loan crisis, and tuna fishing into one of the most dynamic technology-based cities in the United States or the world. Aside from its biotech cluster, San Diego has a separate cluster of about seven hundred wireless communications companies that located here or sprang up here largely because of the presence of Qualcomm, the company that invented CDMA wireless communications. That company's founder, Irwin Jacobs, had obtained experience with the U.S. Navy's communication technologies during World War II and chose to start his company in San Diego. The navy has contributed to the emergence of San Diego as a research center. Its Space and Naval Warfare Systems Command, based in San Diego, spends $2.7 billion a year on research on such key areas as wireless communications and satellites.

The city now boasts a concentration of the finest scientific minds in the world. More winners of Nobel Prizes in the sciences live in San Diego than any other city, and it even has a Nobel Drive, south of the university, intersecting with the Inland Freeway. Craig Venter, considered one of the fathers of biotechnology for his work in sequencing the human genome, is president of the J. Craig Venter Institute and chief executive officer of Synthetic Genomics Inc., based in San Diego. He recently announced that his company had worked with other scientists to create a synthetic genome using computers, a breakthrough in the possible creation of artificial life. William Brody, an acclaimed physician-scientist and former president of Johns Hopkins University in Baltimore, relocated to San Diego to head the Salk Institute for Biological Studies in 2009. The Salk Institute was created by Jonas Salk, who invented the vaccine for polio.

Larry Smarr, former head of the supercomputing facility at the University of Illinois in Champaign-Urbana, came a decade ago to head up supercomputing developments at UCSD. The availability of that computing power in the San Diego area has contributed to the growth of the city's genomics subcluster, which is a blend of biotech know-how and massive computing power. San Diego companies in this field have attracted wide attention: Pathway Genomics announced it would sell self-diagnosing genetic testing kits at Walgreen's (which was blocked by the U.S. Food and Drug Administration, at least temporarily), and scientists disclosed they had used equipment from Illumina, San Diego's largest biotech company, to prove that all human beings share some genes with Neanderthals.[2]

Royston and others also expect that San Diego will emerge as one of the top wireless medicine centers in the country. The Scripps Research Institute recruited a top cardiologist from the Cleveland Clinic, Eric Topol, three years ago, and he holds a key position at the new West Wireless Health Institute, among other roles. This institute is aimed at exploiting the use of wireless communications technology to take X-rays and pictures of patients, monitor their blood pressure or sugar level, and transmit all that information to doctors and nurse practitioners wirelessly. "That is going to revolutionize medicine, and San Diego will emerge as one of the most important centers," predicts Royston.

What was the secret formula for creating a biotech cluster that is helping shape the future of medicine? Aside from the navy, the Scripps Research Institute, today the world's largest independent nonprofit biomedical research facility, has been particularly important. It had its start in 1924 with donations by philanthropist Ellen Browning Scripps, and it promoted the dissemination of its research. Scripps Research was thus an early idea factory, eventually joined by UCSD as it embraced more forward-looking policies regarding its professors and their discoveries.

No single entity was in charge of San Diego's biotech emergence. "It had no guided program," Royston argues. "It grew out of the entrepreneurial talent we had here and the venture capital industry that funded it." Although government funding for research was obviously essential, no government was involved in commercializing the technology. "It was all private money," says Royston. "The real estate people helped by building labs on speculation. But the most important thing is an entrepreneurial, risk-taking climate."

He disputes the argument that federal funding for research alone can explain the emergence of a biotech cluster. "That funding was necessary but not sufficient," Royston says. "Look at Johns Hopkins. It receives about $1.5 billion a year of research funding from the National Institutes of Health, compared to the whole city of San Diego, which gets about $1.2 billion. Baltimore has more funding but far fewer biotech companies. It's obviously not just the research funding." In addition to navy and NIH research grants, San Diego research institutes enjoy funding from the NSF, for an estimated total of $5 billion in 2010.[3]

Nor are San Diego's balmy weather and proximity to outdoor recreation an adequate explanation for the cluster's growth. If those factors were essential, Hawaii would be a technology center, but it is not. And for years many people resisted moving to San Diego despite its climate and relative affordability. "It was an early struggle to attract management talent," Royston says. "In the early days of San Diego, we really had to work hard at getting people to relocate from the East Coast."

Perhaps not surprisingly, Royston argues that the availability of venture capital is one of the most difficult equations to get right but also one of the most important. "The cities that develop clusters are closest to venture capital," he says. "There's a one-to-one match between early clusters and the existence of venture capital." San Diego got started because venture capitalists from the San Francisco area found it accessible. "If you're not within an hour's flying distance of a venture capital firm, it's very difficult to develop a cluster." He notes that another concentration of biotech companies in Rockville, Maryland, has been served by venture capitalists based in New York.

Royston's investment style is one of activism. His firm often provides a temporary CEO to a start-up company if it lacks one, and may take other operating roles to help build a company to the point that it can launch an initial public offering. "We're not passive investors," he says.

Rounding out the biotech ecosystem is the presence of large pharmaceutical firms such as Johnson & Johnson (J&J), Pfizer, Eli Lilly, and Novartis. They attempt to tap into the latest research and also invest in start-ups, sometimes deciding to buy them outright. They are seeking to "mine" the cluster for new technologies. J&J, for example, has employees called scouts who are deeply ensconced in San Diego and who are on the lookout for ideas that the giant company can help nurture. Philanthropists also are particularly active in San Diego, reflecting the surge in the region's wealth in recent years.

Tying the cluster together are groups such as CONNECT, a nonprofit technology organization founded in 1985 that among other things offers free mentoring services for researchers who want to start companies. CONNECT, headed by Duane Roth, a former Johnson & Johnson executive and biotech CEO, has more than two hundred successful entrepreneurs in its ranks who give would-be start-up entrepreneurs the early help they need to prepare themselves to seek financing. CONNECT and a variety of industry associations such as BIOCOM also support conferences, breakfast meetings, annual dinners, educational programs, and a technology hall of fame. Those gatherings and programs allow scientists from different disciplines to meet each other, and also to find investors and business partners. "A good cluster has this kind of support," Royston adds.

It has been a long time coming. The *New York Times* wrote recently, "Ten years after President Bill Clinton announced that the first draft of the human genome was complete, medicine has yet to see any large part of the promised benefits."[4] But that day now is close at hand, and San Diego will have played a large role in making it happen.

San Diego faces certain challenges, as all of America's clusters do—a recent retreat by venture capitalists and angel investors in view of uncertain financial markets, and a shortage of properly trained American workers. But it has nonetheless been a remarkable emergence—and a remarkable life's work for Royston. In an interview with *La Jolla Light*, he described his philosophy as this: "There are three types of people in the world: Those who make things happen, those who watch things happen, and those who ask—'What happened?' Life is much more fulfilling if you are of the first type." He has been precisely that type of individual, to the benefit of a city located far from the lands of his forefathers.

Eric Topol is a Johnny-come-lately compared to Royston, but he will be building on the foundation that Royston helped lay. Born in the borough of Queens in New York City and raised in the Long Island suburb of Oceanside, Topol is obviously another brilliant man. He entered the University of Virginia at just fifteen years of age and rose to become a heart surgeon.

In his professional life, he spent seven years in Ann Arbor, Michigan, fifteen years in Cleveland, where he was a top cardiologist at the prestigious Cleveland Clinic, and three years in Baltimore. He arrived in San Diego in early 2007 with the primary job of becoming director of the new Translational Science Institute at the Scripps Research Institute. He raised $20 million from the National Institutes of Health to launch the institute (the NIH is the research arm of the U.S. Department of Health and Human Services).

In his office, overlooking the tenth hole of the South Course at Torrey Pines Golf Course, he can look out to the Pacific Ocean, where hang gliders attempt to ride the ocean breeze. Torrey Pines is one of the finest golf courses in the United States, but it is a municipal course, so Topol can play a round of eighteen holes for a mere $30, a definite bargain. At fifty-five, he seeks to remain fit also by biking and hiking. "I love it out here," he says.[5] He never wears suits and ties, as he did for years back east, and prefers simple long-sleeved shirts.

The fact that he is allowed to straddle different institutions is also highly attractive. Aside from running the translational institute, he is chief academic officer and part-time cardiologist at

Scripps Health, the largest health system in San Diego, with five hospitals and twenty-five clinics. He also is a professor of genomics at the Scripps Research Institute, and he is chief medical officer of the West Wireless Health Institute. He has two major concentrations, which are widely assumed to represent San Diego's future: genomics and wireless medicine.

On the genomics front, the reason the NIH gave Royston money to create a translational institute is that it is under pressure from Congress and others to demonstrate tangible results from the tens of billions of dollars it has granted to biotechnology researchers over the decades. The NIH receives $30 billion a year from Congress and gives out most of that in the form of grants. In response to the pressure, it has decided in recent years to target more of its money toward translating the huge advances in science into the practice of medicine. "The scientists don't talk to the doctors," Topol explains, echoing Royston. "And the scientists like to work in silos and make fundamental discoveries while doctors are looking after patients and trying to figure out why they get disease or why they don't respond to treatments that are available today. For the most part, these two compartments of the biomedical continuum don't connect very well." He wants to rev up the "discovery engine" to deliver more tangible results.

Humans possess twenty-three chromosome pairs, each representing a contribution from a father and a mother, containing about fifty thousand genes. Scientists have learned how to "sequence" these genes, which consist of combinations of four nitrogen-based chemicals known by the first letters of their names, A, C, T, and G. They are single molecules, and they come in a sequence—AAACTTTTTGGGG, for example. If you map out the molecules, you have sequenced the gene. Think of the body's chromosomes as an encyclopedia consisting of billions of bits of information.

Scientists have been able to decode specific bits of the genome, discovering, for example, what controls hair color. But obtaining an accurate sequencing of the entire genome—the total body of a person's genes—depends heavily on computerization because of the massive numbers involved. Sometimes gene sequences repeat themselves. Sometimes particular sequences of genes appear to have no significance at all. Powerful computers can help detect these patterns and, with human help, achieve an accurate annotated sequencing, meaning one that has been properly sorted out. "We're headed to the day when any person could get whole genome sequencing," says Topol. "It's happening much faster than anyone could have imagined. The race to perform whole genome sequencing is years ahead of schedule. It was predicted that whole genome sequencing would happen around 2015, but we're five years ahead of schedule." Companies are racing to shrink the amount of time it takes to decipher an entire genome to as little as a single day and to reduce the cost from tens of thousands of dollars today to a few hundred dollars.

One bottleneck remains the annotation, or analysis, that must be performed by human specialists after the computer work is over. In one recent case, thirty specialists needed an average of twenty hours each to complete the annotation.

But that bottleneck will be eased, partly through the arrival of better software. "As this becomes low-cost and we develop the software for all this data deluge that's processed, when this becomes practical and we can fill in a lot of the holes in our knowledge, it will be rare for someone *not* to be sequenced," Topol predicts. "You'd know early in life what drugs you shouldn't get and you'd know what doses are best for you and you'd know what liabilities you face in your health and how to prevent these things from occurring." In effect, the information could prevent disease from developing. "In the past few years, we've learned more about the underpinnings of disease than in the history of man," he states.

The ethical issues are significant too. One is whether someone might be discriminated against on the basis of his or her genotype. If a health insurance company knows that a person is susceptible to a disease, it might choose not to insure him or her. The Genetic Information Non-Discrimination Act was passed in the waning days of the George W. Bush administration to prevent that, but certain forms of discrimination by, say, a life insurance company, have not been banned. Another issue is the security of the data, which obviously are intensely private. But overall, says Topol, the benefits outweigh the risks. "It looks like the trade-offs are overwhelmingly positive," he says.

On the wireless front, Topol is chief innovation officer at the West Wireless Health Institute, which is named for Gary and Mary West, a husband-and-wife pair of entrepreneurs who have donated $65 million to the institute. Gary was one of Topol's heart patients. The institute, based in La Jolla, was created in March 2009, so it is just starting its work in earnest. Many experts, including Topol, are excited about how wireless communications could be used to measure and monitor any function of the body—blood pressure, heartbeat, caloric intake, sleep patterns, even a person's mood. That data could be communicated wirelessly to health care professionals or to a family member concerned about an aged parent, for example. "The fact that you can communicate all these continuously, 24/7, means you can convert a home into an intensive care unit," says Topol. Data also could flow the other way, to the patients, reminding them to take medications, for instance. Wireless medicine could dramatically improve the quality of health care, particularly for those who suffer from chronic disease, while reducing the cost of health care. Many patients suffering from diabetes, as another example, would not have to make frequent visits to doctors' offices or clinics.

Some of these wireless health systems are in the early stages of deployment now, but the big payoff is still years into the future. Of the 700 wireless companies in San Diego, Topol says, 150 are working on some aspect of making this wireless health care vision a reality. Two parallel universes—life sciences and wireless—are colliding, with positive outcomes expected. Former Qualcomm engineers are involved in some of the wireless health start-ups, and Qualcomm is an investor in several. The problems facing them include a shortage of scientific research proving that new medical communication devices are safe and effective. And new payment systems also need to be devised because today's health care system does not compensate doctors for electronic consultations with a patient. Overall, the field is still embryonic, but Topol will be pushing for solutions and trying to put new devices into the hands of patients, doctors, and health care organizations.

It's the concentration of intellectual firepower that makes it possible for San Diego to take on challenges such as genomics and wireless medicine. There are four major research institutions—UCSD, Scripps Research, the Salk Institute, and Sanford-Burnham Medical Research Institute. In total, there are fifty institutes, including the Genomics Institute of the Novartis Foundation, and Topol can see many of them by simply looking out his window. "I collaborate with people at every one of these centers where I'm engaged," he says. "There are none of these artificial walls that you might see in other parts of the United States. There's nothing like walking next door to sit down and chat or to go over an idea. That's what's unique about this area. Everything is high-density, within a few blocks. The fact that people are willing to work together sets up a lot of synergies that are hard to replicate."

This is the secret sauce for any technology cluster—creating a culture in which very bright people from different fields and different institutions come from different geographies to collaborate in pursuit of broader objectives. The Cleveland Clinic is a very respected institution, but that city cannot compete with San Diego in terms of the full ecosystem, the complete package. "In Cleveland, you had almost zero life science industry," Topol says. "There was Case Western University and the Cleveland Clinic, but there was nothing else." The patterns of interaction among scientists also were not as fluid. "The camaraderie here may have something to do with the climate or the western spirit," he says. "It's more casual. I rarely wear a tie here. This is all new to me." The ability to create an environment and a culture that attract people such as Eric Topol is one defining characteristic of a successful cluster.

Jay Flatley is one of the small number of people who have had their complete genome sequenced. As the chief executive officer of Illumina, San Diego's largest biotech firm, he has a business reason to promote the spread of his company's wares, which are used to do the sequencing. But it's also a personal story involving choices about what information he wants to have about himself. The Flatley family arrived in California when Jay was a sophomore in high school. Flatley earned a bachelor's degree in economics from Claremont McKenna College and two other degrees in industrial engineering from Stanford University. He went on to become a successful biotech company CEO. At fifty-seven, he runs to stay in shape and occasionally plays golf.

When his genome was sequenced recently, researchers found sixty mutations in his data when compared against a national database that has been built of human gene mutations. These had to be investigated. Many proved to be errors. "Had they been accurate, I would have died young, and I obviously haven't," he jokes.[6] Once the researchers did all the annotation and analysis, they were able to identify a handful of characteristics that he has, and he was already aware of them. He has the sprinter gene as opposed to the endurance gene, which means he's more given to short bursts of activity than to marathons. He has a gene that is associated with slightly higher weight, about four to six pounds above average. Another gene suggests slightly improved potential for intelligence. The most worrisome finding was that he faces a high probability of some type of prostate problem, which he also knew—his father had undergone surgery for a prostate condition.

Some public figures have been quoted as saying they would never want to know what their genome tells them. "They worry and have angst about it," Flatley says. What if their genetic sequence contained seriously bad news? Flatley was willing to take the risk that his sequence would tell him something he might not want to hear. "Alzheimer's is a good example," he says. "If we could tell you that you'd have a higher chance of Alzheimer's, would you want to know that? You can't do anything about it. But I would want to know. It would radically influence my life in terms of the philanthropy I do and in terms of the research programs I take on. For me, it would be empowering."

He predicts the vast majority of Americans will want do what he has done. Right now, the company charges an individual $19,500 for a complete sequencing. A group of five, such as a family, could have it done for $14,500 a person. A patient under the care of a doctor, for whom sequencing would be of clinical value, would pay $9,500. Those prices are going to drop rapidly as Illumina and its competitors keep driving down the costs.

One of the company's core products is a DNA microarray, which is about the size of a microscope slide. It has an incredible forty to fifty million wells on it that can hold genetic material. Flatley likens it to a Chinese checker board that has indentations on it for each marble. One can toss marbles on it and shake it, and the marbles will find a hole, or well. Each of these "marbles" on the microarray contains a fragment of DNA for testing purposes.

The company then uses a combination of techiques—lasers, optics, and high-speed cameras—to take pictures of the genetic sequence. The cameras contain high-speed imaging sensors, mostly made by Japanese companies, that capture millions of images. Those images are then converted into computerized data.

The combination of all these techniques is powerful. "We do have the technology now, with sequencing and arrays, to get at the underpinnings of human disease, to understand how people are similar and how they are different," Flatley explains. This information should allow doctors to know what medications work on which patients, in what dose, and in what combination with other substances. Right now, half the medications prescribed by doctors simply don't work, he says. There are genetic underpinnings, for example, that explain why some patients respond well to codeine and others don't.

It's much the same with cancer. "We're trying to understand cancer at the molecular level and also the genome of the patient," he says. One goal is to understand the nature of cancer itself because it's becoming increasingly clear that there are many different types of cancer. "How do you do a hundred cancer genomes and line them up and deduce what's similar about them and what's different?" he ponders aloud. "What is the molecular reason for a particular cancer? Why does it grow out of control?"

The other goal is to understand a patient's genetics so that chemicals given to the patient to kill the cancer are better targeted to the actual genetic makeup of the patient. Those who have witnessed chemotherapy know that strong chemicals are essentially thrown at a cancer patient to see what works. The science is not yet advanced to the point that specifically formulated chemicals are administered to kill specific types of cancer cells in patients with specific types of genes. Thus Illumina's work holds out great promise for treating cancer.

This type of genetic knowledge will improve the quality of care for many patients, and Flatley says it will also reduce the cost. "This is an opportunity for huge efficiencies," he argues. More drugs these days are being prescribed for patients only after they are tested for a genetic receptor to the medication. "That's the beginning," he says. "Within ten years from now, everyone is going to get sequenced. It's going to be so cheap and so economically compelling, everyone will do it." Hundreds of researchers around the world are working with Illumina equipment to solve genetic mysteries such as the presence of Neanderthal genes in today's humans.

Why is all this happening in San Diego? The original microarray technology was developed at Tufts University in Boston with research funding from NIH. A New York venture capital firm called the CW Group licensed the technology and decided to build a company. The venture capitalists chose San Diego because of the access to so many scientists but also because of the presence of a large pool of trained workers. They recruited Flatley to move from the Bay Area, where he was living. He was attractive to them because he had a track record of commercializing technologies and building successful businesses.

Flatley arrived in October 1999, when the stock market was roaring, and within a month saw an opportunity to take the company public. It had only thirty employees at the time, but Flatley hired a chief financial officer, a vice president of engineering, and a new vice president of manufacturing to round out the management team. Several new executives relocated to San Diego. Illumina went public in July 2000 and raised $100 million. "That was the fuel we needed to really develop the technology," he recalls. The timing was spectacularly lucky because the financial markets soon went into a spin. "Had we not made that call, we would have been acquired by another, bigger company for next to nothing within a year," he says.

Instead, even though venture capital is declining anew and the financial markets are once again roiled, Illumina can play the role of consolidator, buying smaller companies. It has nearly $700 million in sales and a market capitalization of $5 billion. Unless it makes a mistake, the company clearly will survive for the long term. This emergence was enabled by a confluence of factors. "The ecosystem is critically important here," says Flatley. "Access to venture capital was one factor. Another is that the local universities supply so much talent. It's an easy way to get access to technicians to work in the laboratory. And San Diego is such a desirable place that many executives can be relocated."

At a time of deep economic distress, Illumina hired people aggressively in 2008 and 2009. It now has 1,830 people, including 1,000 in San Diego, 300 in the Bay Area, 220 in Britain, 150 in Singapore, and dozens more in other markets. Early investors have been richly rewarded, making roughly ten times as much money as they invested. And the multiplier effect of Illumina's presence is large because many smaller companies are thriving on helping to do the analysis of data that comes off Illumina's systems.

The end result is a company that has some other U.S.-based competitors, but Flatley boasts, "There are few if any international operations that can compete with what we do." About 40 percent of the company's sales are outside the United States. Wealth has clearly been created, and with it high-paying jobs. Microarray technology started with NIH-supported research at a university all the way on the other side of the country. But because San Diego has emerged as such a magnet, it was able to able to draw the idea, the venture capital, and the management talent from other parts of the country. It is no longer a sleepy backwater.

Major companies play key roles in technology clusters—GE and Motorola have been important to A123, GM and Caterpillar have been key players at Carnegie Mellon, and Lockheed and SAIC are important to Orlando's simulation industry. But the connections between San Diego's biotech industry and the pharmaceutical industry are particularly deep.

One reason is that the pharmaceutical industry faces a crisis. Many of its most profitable drugs are going off patent, meaning other companies will be able to make cheaper generic versions of Pfizer's Lipitor, for example, and they will definitely take sales away. At the same time, the research pipelines that these companies have relied on for years are not working fast enough to come up with new drugs, at an estimated cost of $1.6 billion each, to replenish their product offerings. In short, they face potentially catastrophic losses if they cannot come up with new products. So the very model of how they conduct research is undergoing a huge shift.

That's where San Diego comes in. Johnson & Johnson is headquartered far away, in New Brunswick, New Jersey, but it has sought to put down deep roots in San Diego. Overseeing that effort is Garry Neil, an MD and corporate vice president of science and technology.

J&J is a huge, complex animal because it consists of 250 separate operating companies in three different sectors—pharmaceuticals and biotech, medical devices, and consumer products. With $64 billion in annual sales, it says 1 billion individuals use its products every day. It is Neil's job to look outside the company, on behalf of all the operating companies, for new ideas. His office is closely aligned with the J&J Development Corporation, an internal venture capital company. His shop maintains an office in San Diego, where J&J also has a substantial pharma/biotech research facility. Neil also supervises a global network of technology scouts. Overall, the company spends $7 billion a year on research and development, which is more than 10 percent of its total sales. That is considered a very robust R&D effort.

Neil believes that what he sees in San Diego, as well as the Bay Area and Boston, represents the best flow of ideas in the world. "The secret sauce for the United States is the research universities and institutes, which are unparalleled around the world, and our ability to attract the best and the brightest to those universities," he explains.[7] The combination of universities, venture capitalists, and start-up companies results in many "creative collisions," he says. "It's this triple helix effect that you get from venture capital, academia, and industry that is really unique, and it's the special culture that exists in this country and these places," he adds. "This idea that you can be different—you can be an individualist, you can solve the problem—is not nearly as embedded in other cultures."

With his company under pressure, it's not just slick public relations to say that J&J is trying to collaborate with universities and institutes in win-win ways. As research budgets get squeezed, "there is less focus on companies trying to win Nobel Prizes and more on trying to drive innovation, trying to come up with something that people are willing to pay for."

J&J does that in San Diego in a variety of ways. It takes part in research consortia where there is not yet any product, just to maintain relations with key thinkers. His unit invests in smaller companies, and the company's venture capital arm sometimes pitches in—J&J will take board seats and in some cases will license a company's technology or buy the company outright. Neil's goal is to create a portfolio of promising opportunities and to watch them as they grow. That's why he maintains a presence in San Diego. "I like to have people on the ground in these innovation centers, not only visiting from headquarters but part of the community," he says. "They are insinuating themselves into the environment. They're creating some of these creative collisions themselves. When opportunities come up, we can go for them easily. And the talent is coming out all the time on the conveyor belt from the universities. You can hire them for your own labs."

The strategy of collaboration has different names. Some call it *open innovation*. Others call it *external innovation* or *external partnering*. But the goal is the same. As Neil puts it, the goal is to "make the wall between our R&D and academic and small companies much more porous and come up with ways to enhance and finance those collaborations and turn them into products."

For their part, entrepreneurs benefit from having J&J invest in their companies and offering management advice. Left to their own resources, smaller companies might not be able to push their products through hugely expensive clinical trials, so it is better for a larger company to drive that process. Very few can build their companies to the size of an Illumina. The entrepreneurs who sell their companies can become very rich. The relationship between J&J and San Diego is more than a mere marriage of convenience.

San Diego thus has all the attributes of a successful life sciences cluster—universities and institutes, venture capital, small companies blossoming into big ones, and major corporations playing a facilitating role. Yet San Diego does face two challenges, money and people, and these issues also play out on the national stage. And its success paradoxically raises a third issue—who will benefit from its advances on the frontiers of science?

First, the venture capital industry is facing troubles, according to those who follow it on a national level. In 2009, venture capitalists invested the smallest amount of money in technology start-ups since 1997, according to a report from Pricewater-houseCoopers and the National Venture Capital Association.[8] To some extent, it's understandable—investors went overboard on dot-coms and overinvested in the wrong sorts of companies for a period of time. The rates of return were not satisfying, so the investors pulled back. The study found that in 2009 venture capitalists invested $17.7 billion in 2,795 start-ups, which was 37 percent less cash than in 2008.

Venture capital functions as part of a broader financial system. Big institutional investors such as pension funds lend money to venture capital firms with the expectation that the VCs can make a higher rate of return on the money than if the big investors parked their money in Treasury bonds. The VC firms also raise money from wealthy individuals who have much the same motivation. For many years, the gains that VC firms returned to their investors have been taxed as capital gains, not at the higher rates for regular income, another highly attractive feature.

Early-stage VC firms have a symbiotic relationship with angel investors, who sometimes operate together in what are called angel networks, grouping several investors to minimize the risk that each faces. However they are organized, the angels put money into a company when an entrepreneur may still be in the idea stage and may not have built a management team. The angels have traditionally expected that if they nurture the company, VC firms will arrive and invest more money. Farsighted angels might be willing to wait ten years for that to happen. In the best scenario, they assume that VC firms will guide the company until it goes public in an IPO. Everyone involved in the chain of investing will make money. Everyone wins.

But partly because of the upheaval in financial markets, it's more difficult to take a company public these days, which threatens the willingness of investors to take the risk of investing in venture capital firms. "That also discouraged the angel community, which is withdrawing," says Ivor Royston. "They don't want to be stuck." After all, it routinely takes $40 million to $60 million to build a company to the point that it can go public. If angel investors put in $5 million or $10 million in a very early stage, they want to be assured that they can make an exit by selling their shares. If they do not foresee being able to make an exit, they may perceive themselves as "stuck."

Royston has been able to work around the VC malaise by nurturing his companies and attempting to sell them to large pharmaceutical companies. "We're now totally dependent on the pharmaceutical industry," he says.

But over the long term, if conditions don't change and if Congress decides to treat venture capital profits as ordinary income, rather than subjecting it to a lower capital gains tax rate, Royston, an archcapitalist, believes the U.S. government will have to step in. One of his ideas is this: Because the federal government pays for much of the research that universities conduct, why not tweak the formula that was established by the Bayh-Dole Act of 1980? Royston says the U.S. government could specify that universities must invest 5 to 10 percent of the money they make from technology licensing in venture capital firms, rather than simply leaving it in their endowments. Until financial markets regain confidence or the government acts, there is going to be continued uncertainty over investments in high-tech start-ups.

A second major issue facing San Diego, and the country, is this: Who will get the jobs that are being created? It turns out that even though there is a serious long-term unemployment problem in the country, not enough Americans are prepared for the jobs that are being created, says Topol. "The jobs are for people who are trained in sequencing," he explains. "If you're a bioinformaticist or an IT person, have we got a job for you. We can't get these people in fast enough." Help is needed to store data properly and analyze it. That requires some people with PhDs, but also technical people with master's degrees or other postgraduate education. In the wireless medical industry, the need is for more engineers, both electrical and chemical. But the people being hired for these positions tend to be Chinese or Indians educated in their own countries, not American-born individuals educated here.

In short, the American government is supporting research and American universities are pumping out discoveries, but the American workforce as a whole isn't ready to take key jobs. That is not preventing high-tech companies from growing because they have access to the best and brightest in the world, and also can move many functions to where the talent and the markets are located, but it does seem to deprive native-born Americans of some of the gains that their government and university sector are creating with taxpayer dollars. Topol says he sees the gap in skills every day. "We'll interview candidates for these jobs in wireless engineering, for example," he explains. "You don't get too many real well-qualified American people in their twenties. But we get them from the top technical universities of other countries. Their work ethic is extraordinary. They're the ones who get the positions."

To address the problem of American kids not choosing to study and excel in the sciences, Topol joined the Rock Stars of Science program, appearing in magazine ads with Seal, the songwriter and musician. The question in the ads is, who is the real star, the performer or the scientist? The performers volunteer their time to this program. "They believed this was a worthy cause," Topol says. "Rather than all the attention they get, they said, 'Let's get the attention going back to science and math. It's great if you want to listen to my music, but this is hot stuff. You should be thinking about this for your career.'"

Topol notes that Americans are fascinated by television shows such as *American Idol* and *So You Think You Can Dance*, but there is no show entitled *So You Think You Can Compute*. His joke conceals a deadly serious challenge that must be addressed.

A last issue is, who buys the equipment and software that

companies such as Illumina are making? Although the company's emergence is positive for American competitiveness, others in the world can purchase Illumina's equipment to seek genetic insights. The Beijing Genomics Institute in China has bought 138 of Illumina's most powerful HiSeq 2000 systems. That's more than were purchased by all the research institutes in the United States combined. "The risk is that they apply more resources to using our equipment," says CEO Flatley.

He says the Chinese are aiming primarily to genetically improve the breeding of crops and animals, but no one in the United States can control how they use the equipment to, for example, explore the genetic underpinning of human intelligence. Depending on how they use the equipment, it's obvious that the Chinese could gain a competitive advantage over other nations if they make dramatic progress in understanding any or all forms of genetics. "The rest of the world needs to step up and become part of this," Flatley says. "We need to realize that we risk running behind if we don't invest." Even though he is an archcapitalist, he believes that will require some governmental role. "It's certainly a field that will pay back enormously if we make the right investment decisions," he says.

Success, it seems, has a way of breeding the next set of challenges.

★ ★ ★

How Winning Companies Innovate Internally
Corning's Gorilla Glass

THE INTERNAL INNOVATION MODEL of Corning Inc. is different from what some other American companies are pursuing because the company relies on its own idea factory, a research facility called Sullivan Park. But Corning's method of managing ideas as they pass through different stages of development is directly relevant to any American seeking to innovate, whether inside a company or as part of a state or regional ecosystem. And the corporate culture and overall pattern of human interactions that support Corning's innovation also are worthy of emulation.

Corning, New York, is a four-hour drive from New York City, up over the Catskill Mountains and down through the farmland of rural upstate New York. It's a small town of only eleven thousand people nestled in the Chemung River valley. The locals joke that "it takes four hours to get anywhere." And the company's core business might be considered a very mature industry, namely, glass.

But Corning is a quintessential global corporation with a major presence in Japan, Taiwan, China, and elsewhere. It is one of the relatively few major American companies to spend a full 10 percent of its sales on research and development. When Corning makes the right decisions and business is booming, you can feel the prosperity in the nearby small towns and in the shops and restaurants in downtown Corning. When things go bad, little restaurants and art galleries close their doors. That's very different from, say, IBM, which is so huge and spread out over so many geographies that it's almost impossible to make a connection between a decision it has made and the well-being of the surrounding community. Corning is thus a microcosm of what happens in the American economy in a global context.

Corning's path has not been smooth by any means. Amory Houghton founded the company in 1851 in Somerville, Massachusetts, and moved it to Corning seventeen years later. Over the course of its 159 years, its researchers created the first signal glass for railroads, the first lightbulbs for Thomas Edison in 1879, and the first cathode ray tube for the television industry in 1939. Corning also was the maker of CorningWare but saw the profits drain out of that sector and sold that division.[1]

In the late 1990s, the company made a big bet on the glass fiber that goes inside fiber-optic cables and rode the crest of the technology bubble. Analysts on Wall Street even told top management that they should dump every other business Corning had, such as making liquid crystal display screens for consumer electronics and ceramic filters that trap pollutants as they are emitted from automotive and truck engines. Good thing it did not heed those urgings—the fiber-optic market collapsed in 2001 and Corning's sales plummeted, forcing it to close factories and fire workers. Jamie Houghton, a member of the founding family, had to reemerge from retirement to save the company. If Corning had not retained its other businesses, it almost certainly would have gone bankrupt.

After that near-death experience, the company today is fighting back with a new wave of innovation in consumer electronics, including a new product called Gorilla Glass.[2] This innovation is creating jobs, both in the United States and in Asia. The key to this constant reinvention is Sullivan Park, located up on a hill in the city of Erwin, just minutes west of Corning itself.

The story of Gorilla Glass started in 2007 when a small team deep within Corning's Specialty Materials division recognized that the makers of cell phones and other mobile devices were frustrated that the plastic screens on the gadgets were breaking if dropped and were being scratched by keys and other objects. Plus fingerprint smudges were an irritant. The Specialty Materials division was a minor division compared with the Displays division, which was on a roll because it supplied liquid crystal display screens to the makers of televisions and computers all over East Asia. Managers in Specialty Materials were hungry for a hit. One of them was Mark Matthews, today fifty-one, who was a business manager in technical materials. A native of Pittsburgh, he had been with Corning for many years, often in very cutting-edge and risky areas such as pharmaceutical testing or genetic toxicology, areas where Corning has created glass products. He also played a key role in winning key business from Texas Instruments. He was a risk taker.

To find an answer to the problem of cell phone screens breaking, Matthews, as a team leader, asked scientist Ron Stewart to search through the company's archives of glass compositions. These archives are located in a library inside Sullivan Park. There the company has stored all its knowledge from past decades in one place. Stewart discovered Chemcor, a superstrong glass that Corning had unsuccessfully attempted to introduce in 1962 for automobile windshields. Safety regulators demanded that windshields shatter when hit by human heads. But Chemcor was too strong and would not break, so it didn't work for the automotive sector. It languished in the library until Stewart found it again. "He pulled it off the shelf and said, 'This stuff ought to work,'" Matthews recalls.[3]

Matthews became convinced they had hit pure gold. He first needed to run an experimental batch of the glass to put samples in the hands of key customers. The cost was going to be $300,000. His boss, James Steiner, recalls with a rueful smile that when Matthews presented the idea to him, "I must say I wasn't a big supporter of it. I didn't really get the concept of using glass on cell phones."[4]

Steiner, a senior vice president and general manager, acknowledges that there were two issues in his mind: It was near the end of 2007, and the division was about to achieve its budget goals for the year. If Matthews spent the $300,000 on testing the new glass, the division would miss its target—never a good thing in the corporate world. The other problem was that the prevailing orthodoxy in the industry was that the makers of portable devices always have used plastic and would continue that forever. But Steiner acquiesced, and Matthews was able to run the experimental batch. "He took the risk, knowing I wasn't thrilled about it," Steiner says.

One lesson for all Americans is that Corning allows risk taking to be pushed downward to relatively low levels in the company. That is partly due to the culture the company has created in a small town; there are many formal mechanisms for managing innovation, but top management, business line executives, and scientists also have known each other for long periods of time because of geographic proximity and because there is very little job turnover. Steiner, for example, had worked with Matthews earlier when Matthews led the charge on selling Corning products to Texas Instruments (TI) for its successful Digital Light Processing projectors. It was at a time when the fiber-optics business was collapsing, yet Matthews was insisting on using some of those technologies for TI, causing considerable angst within the company. But he persisted, even taking a group of Corning researchers and business unit leaders to China to set up a contract manufacturing production site. Only then did senior management learn about what he was doing.

So Matthews had credibility with Steiner. "He trusts you and gives you leeway," Matthews says. "If you win more than you lose, you get more opportunity." Innovation, it seems, occurs not only as a result of dry data but also as a result of relationships among people, with varying backgrounds and expertise.

To be sure, there is a corporate process that must be respected. Like other top companies, Corning has a rigorous process of managing ideas through a "stage-gate" process where an idea is embryonic in Stage 1, and then as it takes shape it moves to Stage 2. The amount of money the company spends on the idea keeps increasing from one stage to the next. The end of Stage 3 is considered the crucial barrier. If an idea makes it past that, the company is committed to it. Stage 4 is preparation for commercialization, and the product is considered commercialized when it reaches Stage 5. What Corning appears to do better than most is insist that interdisciplinary and cross-functional teams manage the process from very early stages. "If I have a hundred students in a class and I ask them, 'How many of you have a stage-gate process in your company?' about ninety-five raise their hands," says Harvard Business School professor Rebecca M. Henderson, an expert on innovation who has studied Corning, Cisco, Nokia, IBM, and several large pharmaceutical firms. "But if I ask, 'How many of you have a stage-gate process that really works?' only about fifteen raise their hands."[5] Gorilla started in Stage 2, because work had been done on it previously, and it bypassed Stage 3 altogether to enter Stage 4.

The secret of Gorilla Glass is that after it is made, it is subjected to an ion exchange in a salt bath. That means it is soaked in potassium at very high temperatures, several hundred degrees centigrade. The top 40 or 50 microns of glass, on both sides, are the scene of the ion exchange. Sodium ions, which are smaller, leave the glass and are replaced by potassium ions, which are much bigger. It's just a thin layer on both sides, but it makes a powerful difference. Scientists at Sullivan Park joke that it is like having a wall made of tennis balls and then replacing some of the tennis balls with basketballs. The larger objects that are stuffed into smaller spaces make it stronger.

The first production of Gorilla was in a Corning facility in Danville, Virginia. But the company won its first customer in March 2008, and full-scale marketing of Gorilla started in mid-2008. It was time to ramp up production, but where? There was no time to build a melting tank, which melts salts and other chemicals to create molten glass, and Steiner's division couldn't have justified such a large investment on a still embryonic product.

So Steiner approached his colleagues in the much larger Display division and asked for capacity at their Harrodsburg, Kentucky, plant. The Display division was operating at full capacity, so Steiner had to persuade other executives, whose compensation was based on meeting their own targets, to allow him to use one of their melting tanks. He was able to get access. "We went from sampling in December 2007 to full-scale production in May 2008," he says. "We ramped up fast."

This appears to be a key strength at Corning. Even though it can be complex to work out internal bureaucratic turf issues, as at any company, successful divisions recognize that they have to support promising new product launches. "In many companies, Gorilla Glass might get to use the tank one time because the CEO makes the phone call," says Henderson. But after the CEO's attention is diverted, the successful division goes back to its own business, freezing out the upstart. In this case, intervention from CEO Wendell P. Weeks did not have to occur.

Steiner also faced the challenge of drawing in major scientific resources from Sullivan Park, again without putting them on his division's payroll. To do that, he worked with his business technology manager, Xavier Lafosse, who has dual reporting lines, one to Steiner and the other to Sullivan Park. That formal mechanism allowed the Gorilla team to develop relationships with a hundred different scientists.

There was also an underlying social and personal connection between Corning's business units and its researchers. Steiner visited different scientists personally to get them excited about Gorilla. "Our scientists will work where they know they can make an impact and where they're appreciated," he says. "Sometimes it is not just a formal structure. You have to maintain an informal connection."

The reason such major scientific clout was required was that Steiner's team had to put Gorilla through several reformulations, first to be made in Virginia and then to be made in the fusion process in Kentucky. To understand fusion, imagine a house gutter that is open on both sides. Molten glass is poured into the gutter, or trough, and overflows on each side, just the way rainwater would overflow a house's gutter. Pulled by gravity, the molten glass flows downward on both sides but comes together below the trough and is jointed into a single pane. This process creates nearly perfect surfaces and avoids the need for grinding or shining the glass surface. (This represents a *process* innovation, as opposed to a *product* innovation. Innovation comes in many different varieties.)

But then a third formulation was needed. In a bow to environmental sensitivities, the researchers realized they needed to make a "green" version of the glass that avoided the use of arsenic. Going through three innovation cycles in less than two years was impressive.

Throughout this work, Steiner made sure that the scientists attached to the project were meeting face-to-face with possible customers. Scientists "are one of our best commercial weapons," he says. "We have to develop the customers to create demand. It works a lot better if actual scientists do that than if we do it ourselves. In a lot of cases, our scientists have some direct relationship with the customers. The credibility they give us is more than we can grow on our own." Corning finds that if its scientists have strong technical relationships with customers, they can actually anticipate the customers' needs before the customers do.

All the while, Steiner had to build a sales force, much of it in Asia, where the manufacturing of handheld devices is concentrated. He was able to raid other Corning divisions to quickly build up an overall group of about a hundred people. Building a sales force is not often considered part of the innovation process, but if Gorilla was going to become a hit, this infrastructure had to be put into place in a hurry.

As the Gorilla project began soaking up people and resources, other projects had to die, which is one of the toughest challenges in managing innovation in a large company. Corning's response to that problem is to keep a backlog of innovation projects that are unstaffed. "A project team has the responsibility of really giving us the truth of the situation," Chief Technology Officer Joseph A. Miller explains. "If we find that there is an absence of pull in the marketplace, a fundamental flaw in the technology, or if the investment is unaffordable, the project manager is responsible for bringing that information forward. He'll do that if he feels safe, that if we shut it down, those people are going to someplace else within the company. Otherwise, self-preservation kicks in."[6]

The problem isn't so much finding brilliant scientists and researchers as it is creating a climate that encourages the right sort of risk taking. "Some people love taking those chances," says Miller, "but you have to keep it safe."

It all worked. After only a year or so on the market, Gorilla became a hit and was in thirty-five different cell phone models sold by eight companies, including Samsung, LG, and Motorola, as well as Dell's laptop computers. It was selling at an annual rate of $100 million and was projected to become a $500 million to $1 billion business within three to four years, which is significant for a company with $5.4 billion in sales in 2009.[7]

It's impossible not to respect the scientists who are chasing the frontiers of knowledge inside large companies such as IBM, Intel, Medtronic, and Corning. But the people who *manage* the researchers possess their own equally admirable form of wisdom. They have very different attitudes and skill sets that connect them much more to the commercial market. Corning CTO Miller is one of the wisest of those wise people.

He arrived at Corning the summer of 2001 from DuPont, just before the terrorist attacks on September 11 and at a time when the telecom and dot-com bubbles were still inflated. Corning had built labs all over the world in an effort to put its scientists in close contact with customers, which was expensive. The company was spending 70 percent of its research budget on optical fiber and just 30 percent on everything else. Then jets struck the twin towers of the World Trade Center and the bottom of the economy dropped out.

Miller decided to shut down labs around the world except for one in France and another in Russia, and consolidated the company's R&D at Sullivan Park. That ran against the grain of conventional thinking, which favored widely distributed labs. But Miller understood the value of having his key scientists from different disciplines located in a single place. "When you're bringing mechanical and electrical engineers together with chemists and chemical engineers, and with optical physicists and life scientists, and you're working on a system to optically detect a binding event between a photon and a drug candidate, proximity really matters," he explains. He's referring to Corning's efforts to develop glass products that pharmaceutical companies use to test thousands of possible drugs all at the same time.

Making this interdisciplinary process work is key to much of what defines the best in American innovation. As Miller describes it, "Being able to work in a lab next to a physicist who's part of the group, to be able to communicate with him, to routinely have lunch with him, is important."

At the moment of crisis in 2001, Miller also cut back on R&D on fiber optics and gambled on new ideas in consumer electronics. Those are now hitting the market as well. Other hot inventions include a green laser, the creation of which has defied scientists for years. Red and blue lasers have existed, but the full spectrum of color requires some combination of red, blue, and green. The development of a green laser now means it can now be grouped with red and blue lasers to create the full spectrum. As a result, handheld devices could soon project vivid images in color on a wall. Imagine using your cell phone or camera to project a picture up on the wall as you have a conversation with friends or business associates.

Similarly, Corning has developed organic semiconductors that carry a current and therefore information. This is aimed at the market for e-book reading devices. Researchers also have learned to apply a single layer of silicon to glass, which they think will play a key role in organic light-emitting diodes, which some experts believe will change the world of displays, giving them sharper images that require less power.

These ideas are not yet fully commercialized but—combined with other new products in fiber optics such as its ClearCurve product, which can operate around corners—they appear to validate the damage repair job that Miller started. The company today is pursuing more than twenty big innovation projects and more than a hundred smaller ones. Corning's portfolio of ideas "is bursting at the seams," says Miller. "We have more than we can handle."

The company's innovation model is not perfect by any means. If it were, the company would be much bigger and would not suffer from sudden market disruptions. But overall, Corning gets it right. "For a company of its size and complexity, it's exceptional," says Harvard's Henderson.

She says Corning makes its innovation process work because of a "high-conflict, high-respect decision-making process." Corning is able to maintain a balance between systems and process, on one hand, and the right people and the right human relationships, on the other. At one extreme, companies may have the right processes in place but the people involved don't trust each other and don't truly cooperate; at the other extreme, she says, a company can encourage a culture of people who get along very well with each other in personal terms but lack the systems and processes to manage innovation.

Many companies struggle to find this "secret sauce." Researchers at 3M are allowed to take 10 percent of their time to pursue personal interests. But despite the heralded Post-it note, created by accident during an employee's personal time, not a high percentage of the researchers' most creative ideas are turned into actual products. "If there is no place to plug that work in later, it tends to dribble away," Henderson says. "But at Corning, they have a loose-tight balance—looseness when it comes to creativity but then tightness when it comes time to make decisions."

Corning's relative geographic isolation (combined with fresh memories of the telecom crash) helps cement key relationships and break down bureaucratic barriers. Henderson likens Corning's culture to that of Nokia, the mobile phone maker based in Helsinki. "One of the reasons they have been able to move that company so fast and to transition it so many times is that everyone went to the same Finnish technical high school," she explains. Culture, in short, is critically important. And culture is based on human relationships. That's a deep lesson for Americans involved in innovation of any sort.

Who gets the benefits from Corning's innovation? Where are the jobs created? For the Gorilla project, Steiner has tapped a hundred scientists at Sullivan Park on either a full-time or part-time basis. It is supporting their careers to some extent. Yet Sullivan Park is hardly an all-American show—many other nationalities are represented as well. The company can attract high-quality talent from all over the world partly because of its corporate reputation but also because of the presence of recreational opportunities such as the Finger Lakes nearby. The cost of living is modest. School quality is good.

Obviously, the project has also supported employment at factories in Virginia and Kentucky, but of the one hundred people assigned full-time to the project, several dozen are Asians living in Asia—because that's where the manufacturing of cell phones and other mobile devices takes place. Those employees need to be on the ground to sell Gorilla to the companies that do the assembly and manufacturing work. They need to speak the language and understand the culture.

Steiner says Americans have an advantage over their toughest international competitors because of the way they work with customers to achieve breakthrough innovations. "Our German competitors are extremely structured and not as customer-focused as we are," he explains. "They want to take an existing solution and tell people that's the way it needs to be used. We do a better job of working closely with the customer to meet the customer's needs. Our way works if it takes a lot of collaboration with the customer. I think that's what we do best. We do that better than the Asians also."

The key challenge is making sure the products that result from that innovation are made on U.S. soil. "I don't worry about our ability to innovate as much as our ability to maintain a strong manufacturing base, partly because these industries just aren't in the U.S. anymore," he says. "U.S. companies tend to have everything made in Asia. For Dell and for Apple, the entire supply base is in Asia. That forces us, as a component supplier, toward Asia also." One key test was what would happen if demand for Gorilla Glass became so strong that Corning wanted to build a facility just to produce it. With the Harrodsburg plant working at full tilt, the company started converting part of a plant in Shizuoka, Japan, to help meet orders. Does that mean the United States is just a research funnel for others?

Miller seems slightly more optimistic than that. He believes that increased federal spending on research and development could be very positive for the economy, a message he uses to encourage young people to get education in math, engineering, and the sciences. At commencement addresses, he urges them to pursue careers in those fields. "I tell the graduates that this is a very good time to be a scientist," Miller says. "It doesn't feel that way. But if this mimics what happened after World War II, with the creation of the National Science Foundation, or what happened after the launch of Sputnik, with the creation of NASA, there will be a wave of opportunity coming at us."

PART II

ECOSYSTEMS OF THE FUTURE

SIX

★ ★ ★

Smart Energy Grids
Austin Mobilizes to Tap Renewable Energy

BREWSTER MCCRACKEN GREW UP in the sun in Corpus
Christi, Texas, a windy, blue-collar port city on the Gulf Coast
that is home to big oil refineries and chemical plants. In 1980,
at age fourteen, he used money earned from mowing lawns to
buy a photovoltaic motor kit. In his parents' backyard, he also
built a solar water heater from scratch, using a pine box and sheet
metal with copper tubing. A sheet of glass on top of the box captured the sun's power to heat the water. "Something clicked for
me," McCracken recalls.[1]

Three decades later, McCracken is at the heart of Austin's effort to create one of the nation's first smart grids—a municipal
power system that is much more sophisticated and environmentally friendly than anything else that exists today. The goal
is to rely much more heavily on solar and wind power and to
allow individual homes and businesses to generate their own
electricity from solar or wind power and sell that electricity back
into the city's system. This two-way flow of energy is much like
how information flows on the Internet.

It is about much more than being ecologically correct. Mc-
Cracken and the alliance of interest groups he has knit together
hope that creating a smart grid will also create jobs and secure
Austin's economic interests for decades to come. What used to be
a sleepy town has exploded over the years into a city of 750,000
and a metropolitan area of 1.7 million.

But over that time, traffic and energy consumption have also increased dramatically, and many of the semiconductor plants that underpinned Austin's growth have moved offshore. To sustain its growth, Austin's leaders feel they have to try to create a smart grid, which will include smart cars, smart appliances, and all the devices and technology to enable better storage of solar-generated electricity and two-way transmission of electricity. It could serve the dual purpose of easing American dependence on imported energy and creating new industries.

McCracken's Pecan Street Project, as it's called, is an example of how Americans are realizing that being energy-efficient does not necessarily pose a threat to jobs, as traditionally perceived. And it is an example of how Americans working across institutional lines can form coalitions that create wealth while striving to accomplish broader environmental and societal goals. Many cities and regions suffer institutional rigidity. The mayor does not work with the chamber of commerce; the local college president won't speak with business leaders; an economic development agency is staffed with political cronies who don't speak the language of business; and so on. The key players don't cooperate in creating a healthy ecosystem. That's a recipe for economic decay.

To its credit, Austin cooperates across those lines, as evidenced by the Pecan Street Project. McCracken's office is located in a vast building on the northwest outskirts of Austin. It is now part of the University of Texas's Austin Technology Incubator, but it used to be the headquarters of the Microelectronics & Computing Technology Corp. (MCC), which was one of the two consortia set up in the 1980s to prevent America from losing out to Japanese and other foreign competition in the computer field. MCC accomplished its mission and was shut down in 2000; Semiconductor Manufacturing Technology (SEMATECH), the other nonprofit consortium, still exists. Both bodies are examples of the kind of technological cooperation that Austin is known for.

McCracken, forty-three, graduated from Princeton University, where he majored in history, then spent two and a half years on Capitol Hill working for a Texas congressman and also for environmental groups. After that, he came to Austin to obtain a dual degree in public policy and law at the University of Texas. He was a prosecutor in Houston for two years before moving to Austin, where he was involved in commercial litigation.

Reflecting his lifelong interest in alternative energy, he first ran for the city council as a Democrat in 2002 on a platform that spotlighted clean energy, and won. He hosted town hall meetings in 2003 where Roger Duncan, the chief executive of Austin Energy, announced that the utility would grant rebates to individuals and businesses that generated their own solar energy.

He became mayor pro tem of the city council, which was like being lieutenant governor in a state government. Throughout his time on the city council, he learned a great deal about how an electric utility works because Austin Energy is owned by the city of Austin. Its board is the city council. This is a very unusual arrangement and is key to understanding the Pecan Street Project. Very few cities control the utilities that provide them with power. But Austin Energy is the largest such utility owned by a municipality in the country.

It was in March 2008 that important seeds of the Pecan Street Project were sown. McCracken had lunch with Billy J. "BJ" Stanbery, chief executive officer of a company called HelioVolt. That company, founded in 2001, specialized in applying copper indium gallium selenide as thin-film photovoltaic coatings to conventional materials. A roof of a warehouse, for example, could easily be coated with HelioVolt's product and used to generate solar power. Stanbery was certainly promoting his own technology, but he also clicked with McCracken on a deeper level. "He said the approach we were taking with solar was wrong," McCracken recalls.

Essentially, the city was trying to encourage Austin Energy to build a big solar energy plant that would deliver electricity much the same way that traditional fossil fuel plants do. That means they have large facilities located far away from where people actually live and need the energy. The energy has to be transmitted over long distances through an old command-and-control model. The energy only moves one way, from the plant into an electricity grid. "BJ said the real economic opportunity arises when you actually integrate solar into your built environment," McCracken recalls. "Built environment" refers to already existing cities. What Stanbery was suggesting was radical—locate solar power generation inside city limits.

McCracken then called Isaac Barchas, director of the Austin Technology Incubator, to discuss the idea. McCracken was persuaded that having solar energy "distributed," or located within a city, would have the most positive economic impact. A utility cannot burn coal or use uranium in the middle of a city because of environmental and safety worries. "You need to find a way to produce power at the point that it is consumed," he says. "But there are not many credible technologies that allow you to do that other than solar. For solar to work, the delivery model has to significantly change and the energy storage needs to be radically improved." That's one of the big problems with both solar and wind power—figuring out how to store the electricity that's generated at certain hours for use at other peak times.

At their first meeting, McCracken and Barchas brainstormed the idea. "What does success look like twenty years in the future?" they asked. McCracken's answer: "You have thin-film solar on all the buildings. You have two-way wires and the energy storage has to be interconnected. We realized that sounds like the Internet. We realized that the Internet structure was the right way to evolve the energy system."

Crazy idea or solid thinking? It wasn't clear yet. It was partly a question of whether they could get other people to buy into it. So McCracken and Barchas sat down with Duncan, the CEO of Austin Energy, and other players from the Greater Austin Chamber of Commerce and the University of Texas.

Getting the utility in the room was key. Most utilities are regulated by states and consider that state regulators are their key customers because they set the rates for energy consumption and help guarantee profits. Utilities are not known for their consumer focus or their willingness to engage in a somewhat nebulous blue-sky process with academics and visionaries determined to promote forms of energy that disrupt the utility's business model. But because the city owned Austin Energy, the utility went along.

The members of the working group started hashing out what kind of coherent strategy they could create, one that would be efficient with energy but also create jobs. They liked using the word *project* because it harked back to the Manhattan Project that created the first atomic bomb. They wanted to take on equally big challenges. They named their project Pecan Street, which was the original name for Sixth Street, the key strip in Austin's downtown entertainment district.

The working group recognized in the summer of 2008 that they still did not have participation from all the stakeholders involved in the process. And they knew that Austin's efforts in clean energy were not well recognized around the country. To remedy the situation, they did a number of unusual things. First they invited Jim Marston, head of the local office of the Environmental Defense Fund, to get involved. It was a case of strange bedfellows indeed, having the chamber and utility sit down with an environmental activist group.

Even though Marston is an environmentalist, he helped the project attract the interest of IBM, Cisco Systems, and Applied Materials, among other big companies. "We were brought into the project to recruit corporate partners because we had relationships with large national corporations," Marston explains.[2] He had also known Austin Energy's Duncan for years. "He knew that I was going to work for things that were good, not crazy environmental things or things that would bankrupt the utility," Marston says. "If you've been doing this for twenty-five years, people can be comfortable with where your head is."

Of course, the Environmental Defense Fund had its own interests. "Our goal was to create a model that can be replicated across the United States," Marston explains. "We wanted to show that the technology could get amazing environmental benefits. And that if you integrate a smart grid with distributed renewables, with hybrids, with storage, you get even bigger benefits."

Distributed renewables refers to solar or wind power that is generated on a distributed basis, close to where it is used. And when Marston talks about hybrids, he's referring to plug-in hybrid vehicles as part of the system. So the idea that emerged was that if wind (a renewable source) blows primarily at night and there is still no efficient way to store the energy for daytime use, why not use plug-in hybrids? The cars would be recharging at night, when the wind is blowing most strongly. Then the next day, the cars would either be driven or be in position to sell the energy back into the smart grid. This is the kind of practice that might hurt Austin Energy's profitability—if it had to buy energy back from individuals at a certain rate, what price would it pay and how might that affect demand for the energy that it generates at its own plants?

Marston also could see that Pecan Street could be used to address other gaps in how the United States manages its energy. One goal that has eluded energy and environmental visionaries is tying air conditioners and other appliances into an energy grid that can adapt. At times of peak demand, say 2:00 p.m. on a hot day, the system could turn down home air conditioners or turn them off for a period of fifteen minutes to conserve power. Energy prices also could be higher at 2:00 p.m. to encourage homeowners to run their appliances at other hours. But doing that would require smart electricity meters and appliances that also had "intelligence." All in all, it was a grand vision.

In about January 2009, McCracken and colleagues decided it was time to begin a more formal planning process and announced they were launching Phase 1. Twelve different interdisciplinary "action teams" were assembled. Altogether, the process involved twenty senior professors from the university, sixty individuals from corporations, fourteen people from the Environmental Defense Fund, and about forty people from the Austin city government. All contributed their time; no one was paid. They were tasked with digging into the details of each issue, such as storage, and coming up with recommendations. Would this rather awkward process yield any tangible result? It still wasn't clear.

Lenae Hart Shirley, forty, became involved in Pecan Street because the project aligned with her personal interests and with those of her employer, Applied Materials, a multibillion-dollar semiconductor equipment company based in California.

As a child in Austin, Shirley loved the woods, waterfalls, and cave pools, and working to save species such as an endangered blind salamander. The early exposure to environmental causes had a big impact on her. As she explains it, "There's a part of me deep down inside that says, 'People can figure out how to take care of themselves, but who can take care of the environment?' "[3]

After earning a degree from the University of Florida in consumer behavior, she decided that one of her personal life goals should be environmental. She returned to Austin and joined Applied Materials in the mid-1990s. The company's main business was making the highly precise equipment that other companies need to make semiconductors. Shirley was in sales and business development, but something was missing. "Multiple times at Applied, I asked myself, 'How is this going to get me to my goal?' " of improving the environment.

So it was a personal victory for Shirley when Applied decided to expand into the solar industry by making the equipment that other companies would use to produce two different kinds of solar gear, namely, crystalline and thin-film silicon panels. Her new job was to market solar energy to create demands for her company's products.

The Pecan Street Project helped her come even closer to achieving her goals because now she would have a local project on which to concentrate. Each company involved in the project decided which action group it wanted to be involved with; Shirley, and her company, chose to take part in the distributed energy and renewable group. Their mission was to figure out how much renewable energy Austin could generate. They had some financial support from the U.S. Department of Energy, which supported a Solar Cities America study that examined twenty-five cities.

Shirley's team recognized that rooftops alone would not suffice. "We realized there was no one right answer," she says. "We also needed to look at ground mounts, urban wind, waste-to-heat transformation, landfill gas, and geothermal. We were going to have to integrate these technologies together. We turned over every stone and looked for renewable energy solutions." The team met weekly through August.

As pie-in-the-sky as it might sound to a skeptic, there were three very solid business reasons for Shirley's involvement. First, the company was pushing its equipment, which makes solar energy devices. Second, Applied needed to understand how electric utilities think and operate because ultimately they could be large customers, buying power generated by Applied's equipment, which is called SunFab. So Shirley got to know representatives from Austin Energy on her panel. "We're trying to increase the demand for solar all over the world," Shirley says. Right now, Applied sells its solar equipment only in China and other countries outside the United States because there is no demand for it here. (Solar power is not yet viewed as being cost-competitive with electricity generated from fossil fuels.) Applied would not care whether it was a Chinese company or an American company that set up a plant to manufacture solar equipment in Texas, as long as it used Applied's SunFab equipment.

Third, any kind of smart grid that makes decisions about energy consumption and flexible pricing will require more "brains," and that means more semiconductors inside computers. These semiconductors would communicate with each other about how much electricity exists in what part of the grid, where the greatest demand is for that electricity, when it is time to tap stored energy, and the like. These chips presumably would be made by companies using Applied Materials' equipment.

Phase 1 was obviously very complicated work because more than a hundred people were involved in twelve different teams, and they had different interests. Coordinating it all was Mc-Cracken. "He's a visionary," says Shirley. "He looks out into the future and says if we don't do these things today, we'll never achieve what we want to . . . He has so much integrity. The passion shines through. He's a low-key guy, but you get the sense that this man holds our future."

McCracken, meanwhile, was being subjected to the vagaries of politics. He ran for mayor in early 2009. He was endorsed by the local newspaper and successfully raised campaign money. But he lost to one of his colleagues in a three-way race, coming in second. He concluded that the gap was too formidable and withdrew from the race. That could have cast a question mark over the whole project if McCracken had simply dropped out of public life. But he didn't. Instead he decided to devote more time to Pecan Street, even though it was not funded. "I'm sorry he didn't become mayor," says Shirley. "But it's not all a bad thing. Being mayor might have diluted his leadership."

Other questions loomed. Would the project be independent or become part of Austin Energy? McCracken and others decided it should be a nonprofit 501(c)(3). If the project were brought into Austin Energy, it almost certainly would die because it was too much to ask the utility to lead the effort to radically reinvent itself. But who would pay to allow the Pecan Street Project to function? At that point, in the heart of deep economic crisis, it seemed the only answer was the stimulus funding coming from the Obama administration.

In late July 2009, McCracken started putting together a proposal for a regional smart grid demonstration project from the Department of Energy. The department wanted to provide funds for specific sites that were attempting to use the most advanced renewable energy technologies. Environmental Defense helped McCracken with the proposal to test many of Pecan Street's goals at a public-private development project on the 711-acre site of Austin's old airport. The city of Austin had invested nearly $200 million in the mixed-use project, which combined affordable housing with more expensive housing and retail space. Sewers, water lines, power lines, and transformers all were in place on the site, located only a couple of miles from the university and the state capitol. The community had been built as an environmental model, with native landscapes chosen because they consumed less water and were irrigated with reclaimed water. It was also a commercial success. McCracken's proposal was to install solar equipment as part of a smart energy grid combined with new ways of storing energy. The proposal was due by August 26. The project still hung in the balance.

Karl R. Rábago was named vice president of distributed energy services at Austin Energy in April 2009. In many ways, he's a bundle of contradictions—both military tough guy and idealist—but his presence inside Austin Energy is revealing. The utility has to be willing to change its very structure if Pecan Street is ever to prove successful.

Rábago, fifty-one, spent twelve years in the U.S. Army and is qualified in both airborne and Ranger special forces units. With degrees from Texas A&M and the University of Texas law school, he taught thirteen years at the United States Military Academy at West Point, the army's very demanding training institution in New York State.

It sounds like the background of a ramrod-straight military man, but Rábago is also a policy geek with an academic bent. He had stints in the Clinton administration's Department of Energy, worked in the wind power generation field, and served as commissioner of the Texas Public Utility Commission regulating electric utilities. He's been at the intersection of government, think tanks, and private business trying to invent the energy future.

"Why Pecan Street might work," Rábago says, "is that it bears a striking symmetry with the concept of a triple bottom line of sustainability. That is civil society, environment, and the economy as they intersect."[4] Public policy gurus have traditionally argued that the United States can achieve some economic goals, but those may come at the expense of the environment and social goals such as easing poverty. And vice versa—achieving environmental or social goals hurts business. But Rábago thinks the right choice is to try to find solutions that help society, the environment, and the economy all at the same time. "If an idea delivers on all three, it's a triple bottom line winner and we ought to do it," he says.

Energy efficiency is such a winner. "It delivers job benefits and economic growth to all segments of the population, ranging from poor people to rich people," he explains. "It keeps the money in the local economy and it creates jobs. And you avoid pollution locally and it's much better for the environment than any other alternative." Once a utility makes money by being more efficient, it can afford to invest more in clean energy technologies.

For too long, in his view, utilities have run themselves primarily to win rate increases governed by state regulators. That has encouraged them to build big power plants that cost a lot of money. The more capital they spend, the more they can charge.

Previous efforts to deregulate and reform utilities have not worked, in Rábago's view. One trend was to separate the companies that generate the power from the companies that distribute it, breaking up the vertical integration that had long characterized the industry. The thinking was that it would encourage competition and create incentives for companies to invest in more intelligent, cost-effective systems. "But it hasn't happened because we left a lot of artifacts in place," Rábago adds. "We tried to preserve the investments that were made in large capital, so that the large power plants would be taken care of." In short, the existence of so many large power plants—and a system that depends on large, isolated plants—means the industry is not structured in a way that will encourage distributed renewable energy.

Transforming Austin Energy will not happen overnight because, even though it is owned by the city and therefore must respond to what the city council wants, it's not in anyone's interest to put it out of business. If solar and wind generating facilities are going to be distributed, Austin Energy would not own most of those facilities and would not get revenue from the energy they generate. In fact, it would be obliged to buy some of that energy back at a certain price. Smart grids are "anathema to the bottom line" of most utilities, says Rábago, because they have an interest in generating the most volume for the energy they generate from facilities they own.

On the other hand, if a city or region enjoys abundant, cheap energy and if new industries are being born, its economy will boom and demand for all forms of energy will grow, so that would be a benefit for Austin Energy. Figuring out how to change the mix of Austin Energy's business is one of the most important riddles to be solved in order for the Pecan Street vision to truly blossom and help the rest of the United States figure out how to achieve the goals of more efficient, affordable, and renewable energy.

Rábago is clearly charged up about what he's doing professionally. "I'm here," he says, "because I spent twenty years telling people that they ought to do this stuff. Now we're doing it."

The announcement came in November 2009—Pecan Street had won a $10.4 million Department of Energy smart grid demonstration grant for a three-to-five-year project at the old airport.[5] And Pecan Street's board chose McCracken as executive director.

It's right to doubt that a $10 million grant will change the world overnight, particularly when it comes to solar and wind energy. Americans have been talking about alternative forms of energy for decades, ever since the first Middle East oil shock in 1973, and very little has changed. Progress, as some define it, has been blocked in part by the institutional interests of the oil and coal industries and the utilities. It may take decades to completely restructure an energy sector that took more than a century to create.

The lesson of Pecan Street is that when you gather many bright people, with diverse experiences, and their interests can be aligned around a common vision, tangible progress can be achieved even on the toughest issues. This is one of the greatest strengths of the American system—finding ways to encourage and allow people in different institutions to pursue their passions in a common direction. When will Austin know whether Pecan Street was successful or not? "Technology guys move fast," says Rábago. "They don't have a hundred years to haggle. I think we've got a pretty good shot at moving this thing along."

McCracken is connected, in at least two ways, to the most interesting economic development think tank in the country, called Innovation, Creativity, Capital, or IC². It was established by the late Russian immigrant billionaire George Kozmetsky, who in 1960 cofounded a firm called Teledyne, which he built into a Fortune 500 company. He later became dean of the University of Texas's business school and started IC² in 1977 as a separate entity within the university to serve as a catalyst for knowledge creation. His 1988 book, *Creating the Technopolis: Linking Technology Commercialization and Economic Development*, set the intellectual foundation for Austin to consciously borrow from Silicon Valley and Boston's Route 128 corridor. The goal was to turn Austin into a technology powerhouse, and it worked.

The connection to Pecan Street is that IC² is in charge of the technology incubator where McCracken's offices are located. And the Pecan Street Project was based on Kozmetsky's vision of how cities should be linked technologically.

Part of Kozmetsky's philosophy was that economic development can't be driven by a traditional business school. It needs to be an interdisciplinary approach. So IC² has endowed professors all over UT in sociology, public affairs, computer sciences, and management. Similarly, he believed that collaboration among the university, local business leaders, city government, and other constituencies is key to spawning companies. Firms created at IC² include Dell and Whole Foods.

IC² is now run by John Butler, an African American professor from southern Louisiana. He's part of what he calls Louisiana's black bourgeoisie and is the fourth generation of his family to receive a college education. Thirty-four years ago he came to Austin to work at IC^2 and grew very close to Kozmetsky, who eventually handpicked Butler to take over.

Butler, in his fifties, is an expert on technology diffusion, like Kozmetsky. But he approaches the subject from a different direction. On his wall is a framed certificate acknowledging his father as a county agricultural agent in charge of helping farmers improve their agricultural practices. Butler says he also admires Booker T. Washington, who was born in 1856 into slavery in Virginia. After the Civil War, Washington became an educator at Tuskegee Institute in Alabama, and believed in providing knowledge and technology to former slaves. In Butler's view, both his father and Washington played key roles in disseminating knowledge into the agricultural sector. "The model is how America took the research from the labs and fed the world," he says.[6]

Today, the burning imperative is not agricultural growth but rather using technology to create jobs and wealth. "What America has done in recent years was to move funding for innovation from private labs to universities," he argues. It's true that major companies have cut back on their research. "So now we have these large research universities, which have offices of technology transfer and commercialization," he notes. "How do you take the innovation to create wealth?"

This is what he means by *diffusion*—how technology spreads. And he believes the key ingredient in diffusion is how a local community invests its wealth. "You can't have the research sitting there in the lab without the individual wealth to commercialize the ideas," Butler continues. "Wherever I go, I want to meet the wealthy people. I'm not interested in what the governor has to say. What we have learned here at IC^2 is the tremendous role that established wealth has in investing in new ideas."

That's what happened in Austin—Kozmetsky created a capital

network offering seed money to start-ups at an earlier stage than most venture capital firms are willing to do. As Butler puts it, "He went to the wealthy people and said, 'Take a chance on these kids. Maybe you'll make some money on these computers and software.'" And of course, they made billions on companies such as Dell. Kozmetsky created what is called the Texas Capital Network, and Butler manages it today.

He also oversees $280 million in start-up funds as part of the Governor's Fund for Emerging Technology. That's a huge amount of money for a state start-up fund, but the state government knows it cannot evaluate business ideas. So it leaves the decision making in the hands of Butler, who creates committees of academics and business leaders to make decisions about which ideas to back. The money goes into four areas: biosciences, clean energy, wireless communications, and information technology including software and semiconductors.

Many of the firms he invests in take root at the Austin Technology Incubator, which has incubated 150 companies and raised $750 million for them. Surviving companies today have $1.5 billion in revenue and ten thousand jobs in Austin. Kozmetsky obviously built a multifaceted powerhouse for innovation, one that endures. Whether the story is told by a Russian immigrant billionaire or an African American professor from Louisiana, America has huge potential to create wealth. Austin is proof of that.

SEVEN

Gearing Up the American Export Machine
North Carolina Builds Its High-Tech Exports

NEARLY EVERYONE AGREES that one important key to creating economic growth, wealth, and jobs is encouraging
smaller and medium-sized American companies to become more
active internationally. After all, 95 percent of the world's population is outside the United States. Companies that export typically
pay higher wages and stay in business longer. America has 30 million businesses, yet less than 1 percent export or engage in international strategies, according to the U.S. Department of Commerce.
Although that 30 million includes mom-and-pop businesses that
never would be expected to export, there is huge untapped potential even if the number of companies with the potential to
export is just 3 million, a tenfold increase over today's number.
President Obama has declared that his administration wants to
double U.S. exports over the course of five years, creating 2 million jobs.[1]

But the American export promotion and financing system
is fragmented and disorganized compared with the ecosystems that the Japanese and Germans have built.[2] U.S. system
technology licensing rules, the subject of constant infighting
among the U.S. Departments of State, Commerce, and Defense, also impose disincentives against exporting.[3] Economists in New York and Washington have long argued that the
only way to increase exports is to drive down the value of the
dollar, which has the effect of making American manufac-

tures cheaper abroad. Others advocate enacting new free trade agreements.

But the real challenge is at the state and local levels, where agencies have the primary responsibility of encouraging new entrants to enter the export game and helping existing small exporters to expand. As in technological clusters, that requires improving institutional alignment and collaboration and improving the flow of information to lubricate the wheels of commerce. That can be consciously modeled; it does not have to happen by accident or at the whim of foreign currency exchange rates. Creating an export ecosystem also depends on having experienced people in the right positions.

North Carolina has traditionally been known for tobacco, textiles, and furniture. But as those industries have gone through regulatory and economic upheaval and lost tens of thousands of jobs, the state has been obliged to make a push into higher-technology goods—and the ability to export some percentage of those goods has been essential to sustaining the growth of those industries and the jobs that go with them.

Unlike some other states and regions, North Carolina has developed and maintained a robust ecosystem to support the go-global efforts of its small entrepreneurs. The state, which consists of very different regions based on geography and industry mix, has seven economic development partnerships that perform a variety of functions at the grassroots level. One is to connect the chief executives of small firms interested in exporting with the state's Department of Commerce, which maintains seven offices around the world, in Shanghai, Hong Kong, Toronto, Frankfurt, Tokyo, Seoul, and Mexico City.

Small business centers at community colleges also refer CEOs to the state. The state cooperates, in turn, with the U.S. Department of Commerce and its U.S. & Foreign Commercial Service, the Small Business Administration (SBA), and to some extent the Export-Import (Ex-Im) Bank, which is designated to provide insurance and export financing. The U.S. government's presence is light; the Ex-Im Bank representative assigned to North Carolina is based in New York City, for example. But all the agencies, from the local regions up to the state and the feds, cooperate in providing information to small-company CEOs about trade shows in foreign capitals, playing matchmaker with potential distributors and customers, training CEOs how to ship and insure their goods, helping them travel to foreign capitals, translating their companies' sales materials into local languages, hosting receptions at U.S. embassies, and the like.

A key person in making it happen is Jean Davis, originally from Boston, who runs the state Department of Commerce's export promotion services. She was originally the CEO of a small biotech company that went global using the state's services. After selling her company partly on the strength of its international sales, she took over the state's export promotion efforts three years ago.

The different governmental players involved in North Carolina's exports have a monthly telephone conference call during which they compare notes on specific companies trying to start exporting or to expand their exports to new markets, and what assistance those companies need. This helps smooth the way for the agencies to cooperate in providing what a company needs. "They seem to have it wired and greased pretty well," says Paul Clayson, a chief executive officer whose company, nCoat, is based in Whitsett, about an hour and a half west of Raleigh. Although different agencies are involved, "it seems like a single resource," he adds.[4]

That's in sharp contrast with export ecosystems in other states, where agencies often are poorly staffed or else staffed with political appointees who know little about international trade. In those cases, the agencies sometimes send CEOs on wild-goose chases for information and advice. Or else they don't cooperate with each other because they worry that another agency will "steal" their clients, namely, the CEOs. In other cases, state and federal agencies do not communicate at all.

There are gaps in North Carolina's ecosystem, to be sure. Large money-center banks and even regional banks have retreated from providing small companies with letters of credit, which permit the companies to get paid when they put their goods on a ship or plane. As a result, most companies are not even troubling to ask the banks for help and are shipping their products on the basis of trust. Early-stage venture capital, which can be useful in helping a small company gear up production to meet large foreign demand, also is in short supply compared with Boston, Silicon Valley, Austin, or San Diego. "General lending is drying up," says Davis. "I'm hearing that from companies whose CEOs say, 'I have this order from overseas. If I had the capital to produce this stuff, I could make the sale.' "[5] Sometimes they simply cannot find the capital and the sale is lost.

But overall, North Carolina is a positive example that speaks directly to the national debate about exports. The tale of two North Carolinian exporters shows how a public ecosystem supports their commercial efforts. Michael Zapata III, from Raleigh, North Carolina, is exporting nanotechnology tools. On the eastern side of the state, across I-95 down toward the Atlantic Ocean, in the small town of Greenville, Craig Hamilton is exporting software used to test the expiration date of pharmaceutical products. The software goes to more than twenty countries, particularly Germany, South Africa, Israel, and lately, Brazil.

Each of them has what might be called a niche product, but the key to understanding North Carolina's and indeed America's export possibilities is that U.S. companies already dominate many of these niches on a global scale and could dominate thousands more.

Michael Zapata spent twenty-one years in the U.S. Army, many of them as an attack pilot flying Apache helicopters. But now he has carved out a unique civilian role in Raleigh—he's entrepreneur in residence at North Carolina State University, he's an angel investor in companies emerging from the robust laboratories in Research Triangle Park and from North Carolina State, he helps smaller companies get started, and he consults for larger companies and foreign governments about innovation and growth strategies.

Protochips is a new company founded by three men working toward their PhDs at North Carolina State as part of midcareer transformations. In their mid- to late thirties, they were studying electronics. Led by David P. Nackashi, now the company's CEO, the three discovered that the electron microscopes they were using to examine new materials and other substances had an inherent flaw—they merely took snapshots of reactions at the atomic level that could be viewed only in retrospect. This is an obvious simplification, but if researchers mixed two substances and heated the mixture to observe how heat affects it, they would have to wait for the reaction to end, then move the results to the microscope to examine what happened.

In Zapata's terms, they could only do "postmortems," or examine the results of an experiment after it is over. "Wow, this is kind of archaic," the PhD students concluded. Wouldn't it be better to have a system that allowed scientists to watch the interaction of atoms in real time, more like a video camera than a still camera? That would have the added advantage of watching the reaction in its natural environment, not after it had been moved.

So they invented the technology to do that. The key was a semiconductor device that they were able to develop in a clean room at the university. Their research was conducted on the side, so the university never owned their intellectual property, and the trio won U.S. patents for their invention, which builds laboratory functions onto the semiconductor chip. It thus allows two types of devices—scanning electron microscopes and tunneling electron microscopes, each costing more than $1 million—to observe experiments at the nano or atomic level in real time. The trio's semiconductor was packaged with other hardware and software to create a system that the fledgling company wanted to sell. Aside from companies making solar panels, batteries, composite materials, coatings, and other products whose composition is critically important, the other logical markets were U.S. national weapons labs and research institutes and universities.

The trio needed someone who had actually created a company before. So they turned to Zapata, the entrepreneur in residence. He helped them package their technology into a product, create a management structure, and start to raise capital. As he had with other companies, he invested some of his own money into the venture in early 2009. Zapata's title is executive chairman, and he expects that once he has helped build the company to the point that it has momentum, he will leave, almost certainly earning a profit on his investment. Zapata, forty-two, has invested in thirty companies and attempted to nurture them.

Right now, Zapata is working on developing Protochips' international sales channels, which means exports. The company does not disclose its earnings, but it is still quite small, with about a dozen full-time employees. Sales are growing rapidly, and the company is self-funding and already profitable. International sales are one reason the company has been able to achieve profitability so quickly, avoiding a long valley of death. Some 35 to 40 percent of its sales were offshore in 2010, and more than half will be outside the United States by 2011.

One step was finding a distributor in Japan to handle sales throughout East Asia. The state and U.S. Departments of Commerce helped make the connection, as they have for previous companies that Zapata has managed. Working together, rather than competing with each other, the state and federal agencies helped Protochips research the right companies to do business with in Japan. They helped set up initial visits, arrange meetings, and locate places where Protochips executives could hold meetings. They performed other crucial functions such as helping translate sales materials and documents into the Japanese language. Because both the state and federal agencies employ Japanese nationals, the quality of translation was excellent. A bad translation can doom any presentation.

Both state and federal agencies have suffered some budget cuts, so they are not doing as many of the more expensive trade-promoting events such as large trade missions or paying entrepreneurs to travel to trade shows. "Any kind of financial support isn't going to happen," Zapata says. "But they've got people on the ground in these countries who will help you out."[6]

Thanks to that help, Zapata negotiated the terms for a large Japanese manufacturer of microscopes to carry his company's product. The agencies also helped him obtain legal clearances to export Protochips' products, win certification in Japan, and resolve complicated tax issues.

Isn't it dangerous to export a high-tech product to a part of the world where good ideas are often copied? Zapata says that not all small companies should consider exporting to Asia through a distributor, but it made sense for Protochips. "I try to stay involved in deals where there is something that allows you to maintain a defensible position in terms of intellectual property, which is a barrier to entry," Zapata explains. "Otherwise, you sell one and then your product is replicated." No one in Asia or Europe makes a device like the Protochips product, and it would be difficult to imitate—and also easy to detect.

"We also saw large markets outside the United States that were growing rapidly, and we could leverage existing distribution networks so that we did not have to go to the expense of building a distribution network ourselves," he adds. In the best of all possible worlds, an exporter has its own employees on the ground in at least a few countries to maintain the sales network and offer service to customers. Protochips might have been able to do that, Zapata says, if it could have raised early-stage venture capital, but that's something North Carolina lacks. So they had to take the shortcut of piggybacking on an existing manufacturer.

The reason to go through all the trouble of exporting is that it's a way to grow faster. "If we wanted to get the same amount of growth in the United States that we're going to get in Asian markets, we would have to raise and invest more money to do that," Zapata says. "We would have to build out a stronger distribution channel. But in Asia you have distributors who can bear more of the cost of distribution, in return for giving them more of your profit. You can add that growth." As Protochips grows and hires more people in North Carolina, the wisdom of the combined state and federal support will become evident.

Craig Hamilton was born and bred in eastern North Carolina, which he believes might as well be considered a different state from western North Carolina. Greenville, a town of about seventy thousand, is located in a mostly agricultural part of the state close to the ocean, far away in both distance and psychology from the high-tech companies of Research Triangle Park and the bank skyscrapers of Charlotte, far to the west.

But even though Hamilton might appear to be just a good ol' boy, he has done two sophisticated things to keep his H&A Scientific in business and to attempt to nurture it into becoming a larger business through exports—he has used the Internet to his advantage and made clever use of the governmental export infrastructure that's in place to help him.

Hamilton is a chemist by training and went away to work as a lab chemist for what is today GlaxoSmithKline. It was not a glamorous job, but it taught him enough to come home in 1992 and create a company that makes software to track all the data that pharmaceutical companies have to collect to establish an expiration date for a particular drug. Even a bottle of aspirin must carry an expiration date. Every different formulation of a medicine has to be tested for when it will no longer be effective. The method of packaging also matters—sometimes pills will last longer if there are more of them in a bottle rather than fewer. The company's software tracks tons of this data during clinical trials and then calculates an expiration date in a way that the U.S. Food and Drug Administration (FDA) finds acceptable.

Sales are about $1 million a year, but 2009 and early 2010 have been tough because many of the small pharmaceutical start-ups that would have bought his software either have gone out of business because their venture capital dried up or were forced to sell themselves to bigger companies. From a high of fourteen people in 2007, the company now employs nine, including Hamilton.

The company has created a Web site (www.hascientific.com) where it displays how its product works in English, Spanish, German, French, Polish, and Portuguese. Potential customers can test the software in this variety of languages and then hit a button to translate it all into English, or any of the other languages, for possible submission to the FDA or to the regulatory authorities in their own countries. How could such a small company in the boondocks develop that linguistic sophistication? Hamilton turned to the Pitt County economic development group and found a German woman who'd married an American military man who was reassigned back to a military base in North Carolina. She manages some of the company's German-language Web site functions, although Hamilton is studying German and can read it. For Spanish-language markets, Hamilton found a Colombian woman who relocated with her family to North Carolina.

Hamilton uses Skype or e-mails to speak with customers and possible new customers, and he can conduct demonstrations using WebEx. "I can do demos while I'm sitting here in Greenville," says Hamilton.[7] The company also has beefed up its Facebook profile to build social connections with foreign customers and attempt to draw them in on a more personal, rather than purely business, basis. All these tools did not exist a decade ago and are one reason that such a small company can sell its software in so many countries. "There's no way we could do this without the Internet," he says.

Exports still represent only about 10 percent of sales, and in view of the troubles in the U.S. economy, he is getting much more serious about expanding sales offshore. He made one trip to South Africa by himself to gear up exports and also has traveled to Israel. But county officials introduced him to Jean Davis's office, and since then the state has helped him expand more rapidly than he could on his own.

"Whenever we go to trade shows," he explains, "people from Europe will come up and say, 'This is a nice-looking software package. But how can we buy it when you don't have an office in Europe to support it?'"

He used to try to persuade potential customers that they didn't need a local H&A presence, but it rarely worked. To address that problem, the state's office in Frankfurt recently helped him find a company in that city that will answer phone calls from customers in the German language, do mailings, and provide some service to customers. That costs only 600 euros (about $1,000) every three months. The state also helped Hamilton open a bank account at Commerzbank in Germany so that European customers can pay for his software in euros, which spares them the need to convert their currency into U.S. dollars. "You have to be somewhere in Europe, and Germany is in the heart of Europe," he says.

The state has also introduced him to federal programs. In the spring of 2010, he went to Brazil as part of a U.S. Department of Commerce program called Tradewinds. Hamilton paid a modest fee (about $1,900) to be included in the trade show, which spotlighted many small exporters. It was a bit overwhelming because the country's capital, São Paulo, has nearly twice as many people as the entire state of North Carolina, he jokes. Brazilian companies are trying to become more sophisticated about how they sell pharmaceuticals in their own country and in the United States, so they were attracted to the Portuguese-language capabilities of Hamilton's software and to his company's sales materials, which the government helped him translate into Portuguese.

The roles of county, state, and federal agencies thus have been crucial to his efforts to find momentum in exporting. For Hamilton, the expression once used by the Japanese seems appropriate—"export or die." He has to make continued export inroads if he is going to survive the U.S. economic crunch. He owns 74 percent of the company himself and it is currently in the black, but not by much. "We have to earn our money to continue to exist," he says. "There are no deep pockets anywhere."

He thinks his international sales are going to increase rapidly, and when that happens he will have to start hiring again. He likes the idea of becoming a $20 million company. "I'm an eternal optimist," he says. "You have to be."

The state's Jean Davis took a job with IBM in Research Triangle Park in 1992 and has stayed in North Carolina ever since. Now forty-two, she has directed the state's export promotion efforts for the past three years. She did not create those programs, but she has helped shape their culture and overall effectiveness. Even though her department has suffered budget cuts, as the vast majority of state agencies have, she was able to open a new office last year in Shanghai. One reason for the relative consistency of her office's purpose is that North Carolina has been led by Democratic governors for many years. So the governor's mansion has not had a change of party leadership, which might have resulted in drastic changes to the state Department of Commerce. Overall, some twenty-five people work for Davis at home and abroad. Important is that all of those people have had private-sector experience and understand many different technologies.

But they alone would not be very effective if it were not for the state's system of pushing funding and decision-making clout down to the regional economic development partnerships. State offices in Raleigh or Charlotte are far removed from the small towns where most small companies are located. These regional agencies "talk to customers every day," Davis explains. "They know what clients are going through."

The regional agencies and the state do a great deal of what might be called missionary work—trying to convert nonbelievers into believing that they can be successful internationally. "The idea is to get them in the door, get them thinking, and then get them on a plane," says Davis. "That involves a lot of handholding."

Aside from the services that Zapata and Hamilton used, the U.S. Department of Commerce offers other assistance such as its Gold Key Service. There are several levels of this service at different costs. For a fee, the department's Foreign and Commercial Service will organize meetings in foreign capitals and host receptions where exporters can make presentations to possible customers that foreign nationals working in the embassies have identified and invited. The U.S. & Foreign Commercial Service also has a much more extensive presence internationally than the state does and can supply information about distributors and customers in countries where the state does not maintain offices.

But most small exporters say it takes experience and size to deal with the federal government, which is why they prefer to deal with state representatives, at least in the beginning stages of their go-global efforts. Over time, Davis introduces her small-company CEOs to federal agencies. Her department and some federal agencies will even make joint calls on clients and share the clients, rather than fight over them. "If the client says they want to do business in Brazil and China, I say, 'We'll help you in Brazil,' and the U.S. Department of Commerce says they'll help you in China. We're happy with that."

The state also attempts to explain how the Small Business Administration makes small business loans and how the Ex-Im Bank insures export loans made by local banks. "Your average person doesn't know about SBA and Ex-Im," she says.

There are other pieces in the state's export ecosystem—programs to train CEOs in how to export and mentor them, for example. Helping tie all of it together is the District Export Council, which is a blend of the governmental players and private-sector CEOs interested in exporting. As with most successful ecosystems, there is no one person and no one agency that makes it successful. It hinges on collaboration.

It has worked. Davis's department claims responsibility for some $158 million in North Carolina exports in the fiscal year 2010. The state as a whole will export $25 billion of goods and services, making it one of the top fifteen states in the country. Plastics and chemicals are the number one industry group, followed by computer gear and software. The CEOs who have used the export services argue that they are an entirely legitimate role for government. "If you can have one person in a country, he or she can support fifty companies back in the United States," says Zapata. "These things make a lot of sense."

The export of agricultural goods and other raw materials are important to North Carolina and many other states, but the real key for the future of the American economy lies in manufactured and higher-value-added goods because jobs in those industries require higher levels of education and thus pay higher salaries.

Some pundits lament the fact that "America doesn't make things that the rest of the world wants." That's true in the realm of consumer electronics and personal computers. But in dozens of other sectors, American companies have carved out niches that they exploit globally. Aside from nanotechnology and software, it is worth listing just a few—medical devices, wheelchairs, conveyor belts, advanced robotics, lighting fixtures, special concrete, scientific testing devices, filters, chemicals and plastics, irrigation systems and agricultural equipment, mining equipment, aircraft parts, and small engines. If the export valves could be opened for more companies, as they are doing in North Carolina, the effect on jobs and wealth creation could be huge.

Skeptics also argue that, yes, you can increase exports from a handful of specialized companies, but what could that possibly mean in the overall context of the whole U.S. economy? The answer is that the niches may be narrow, but when added up, they represent formidable possibilities. If a million U.S. companies grew in size from, say, $10 million to $100 million a year in sales, that would have major impact on employment.

Some small American companies can go international without anyone's help. Perhaps the CEO had experience in a larger multinational and already knows the international ropes. Or perhaps the CEO is foreign-born and therefore has cultural and linguistic connections with export markets.

But the majority seem to need help, at least in the early stages. That's why export ecosystems are so important for America's hopes of creating jobs at home while maintaining strong positions in many promising technologies around the world.

EIGHT

Bring It Home
Atlanta Lures Back Manufacturing from Abroad

FOR YEARS THE NCR CORPORATION simply followed the pack. Like many other large U.S. manufacturing companies in the past couple of decades, the maker of automated teller machines (ATMs) relied heavily on offshoring and outsourcing to trim costs. By making much of its equipment in cheaper off-shore locations in Asia and by hiring Singapore's Flextronics International Ltd. to make some of it in a variety of locations, NCR could slash millions of dollars in plant expenses and be reasonably certain that its ATMs met quality standards.

But it was not as ideal an arrangement as it first appeared. The collaboration with outsourcers became "an enormous and costly exercise," in the words of one manager. Engineers had to jet around the world to sort out production glitches and design changes. The company also was concerned that outsourcing to others and making its own products in foreign lands meant that it was not able to respond quickly to the needs of its largest and best U.S. customers. Client banks such as JPMorgan Chase and Bank of America were engaged in intense competition with each other and were pushing NCR (which once stood for National Cash Register) to introduce products that would give them an advantage. The underlying technologies—imaging, computing, and high-speed communications—all were evolving rapidly.

What the banks wanted were higher-end products that scan cash and checks and do not require a deposit slip, sparing customers from having to stuff a deposit envelope. Introducing those products required different departments within NCR to coordinate with each other more smoothly and also with customers. "On the very high end, you're getting into some highly innovative products that require quite a bit of involvement by different constituencies to bring to the market successfully and quickly," says Peter Dorsman, the company's senior vice president in charge of global operations. "That's when we started thinking about, 'What's the right way to think about this? Is there a better way?'"[1]

The answer ultimately proved to be yes. NCR made a major shift in manufacturing strategy for its sophisticated machines.[2] In 2009, the company decided to leave some lower-end manufacturing offshore but opted to move its most sophisticated lines of ATMs from its plants in China and India, and from a Flextronics facility in South Carolina, and instead manufacture the machines itself in a former battery plant in Columbus, Georgia, not far from its service and support centers and its newly relocated corporate headquarters. "We take our cue from our customers," says Dorsman. "They are heavily involved in the development process. And with this new approach we're taking, we can get innovative products to the market faster, no question."

The state helped identify and train two hundred workers for the plant, which is still in the process of increasing production, and helped to create an ecosystem of university training, suppliers, and logistics experts. "I think you'll see more of this occurring," says Dorsman, fifty-five, a native of Albany, New York. He says he has been contacted by dozens of U.S. companies studying whether they should make similar moves. "You'll see a lot more people returning manufacturing to America."

One major attraction for NCR was the willingness of the state of Georgia and its university system to work with NCR to train workers and help create an ecosystem that would allow the factory and associated functions to become profitable, as well as capture the innovation sparked by engaging with university supply chain and logistics experts. The company also moved its headquarters from Dayton, Ohio, to the Atlanta suburb of Duluth, so many of the company's key functions for the U.S. market are now concentrated on the fringes of this sprawling metropolitan area.

NCR's change in direction has raised the possibility that U.S. manufacturers are getting serious about "backshoring" some of the production they shifted overseas in the wholesale offshoring movement that started in earnest in the 1990s. General Electric Company chief executive Jeff Immelt attracted attention for remarks he gave to a West Point leadership conference calling for U.S. companies to make more products at home. Demonstrating Immelt's commitment, GE announced in the summer of 2009 that it would build two new plants in the United States—a factory in Schenectady, New York, to make high-density batteries and a facility in Louisville, Kentucky, to produce hybrid electric water heaters currently made in China.

Caterpillar, the big construction equipment company based in Peoria, Illinois, also says it is tripling its U.S. production of construction excavators by consolidating production from a factory in Akashi, Japan, and one near Chicago into a U.S. site that has not yet been determined.[3] Other work will be shifted to Japan so that workers there will not be displaced—that would violate Japan's social norms against layoffs. But its decision was another suggestion that backshoring could gain ground. "After a decade of rapid globalization, economists say companies are seeing disadvantages of offshore production, including shipping costs, complicated logistics and quality issues," the *Wall Street Journal* wrote. "Political unrest and theft of intellectual property pose additional risks."[4] It quoted a representative of the Manufacturers Alliance, a public policy group, as saying: "If you want to keep your supply chain tight, it's hard to do that with a 16-hour plane ride from Shanghai to Ohio."

Whirlpool Corp., the big appliance manufacturer, is spending $300 million to upgrade its domestic manufacturing facilities, which the *Wall Street Journal* described as part of a "shift by even export-driven U.S. manufacturers away from low-cost overseas locales in favor of rationalizing domestic operations to boost productivity."[5]

Similarly, Intel has signaled that it wants to maintain strong connections with American centers of innovation. In February 2010, it announced a $3.5 billion initiative to support investment in clean technology, information technology, and biotechnology.[6] The company's Intel Capital arm, a kind of internal venture capital fund, announced it would invest $200 million and would be joined by twenty-four venture capital firms to bring the total investment to $3.5 billion over two years.

If companies do get serious about investing more in America, it could have huge impact on job creation. The Federal Reserve reports that U.S. companies are holding more cash and liquid assets than at any other point on record, an incredible $1.84 trillion.[7] Many are hesitant to spend on hiring or expansion amid doubts about the strength of the recovery. Could political leaders, eager to create jobs, unlock those treasure chests with the right mix of policies?

Now may be the time. In addition to the factors cited by the *Wall Street Journal*, increases in raw material prices in China have discouraged some U.S. companies from manufacturing there and shipping the products across the Pacific Ocean. Wright Engineered Plastics Inc., a Santa Rosa, California–based maker of injection molds, for example, has expanded its West Coast plants and decreased its use of Asian facilities because many of its key customers have shifted their own manufacturing operations back to the United States in light of prohibitive increases in the prices for raw plastic in China.

Some companies are modernizing their U.S. plants to outperform Chinese facilities. For example, Diagnostic Devices Inc., a maker of blood glucose monitoring systems in Charlotte, North Carolina, announced in August 2009 that it was moving the manufacturing of its Prodigy line of audible glucose monitors to North Carolina. That ended a five-year agreement with a contract manufacturer in China under which Diagnostic Devices sent components overseas and then had the finished devices shipped back to the United States. By automating its U.S. factory with robots and other high-tech gear, and by taking advantage of lower shipping fees, Diagnostic Devices reduced its production budget by 40 percent. And there was an added bonus, according to a company spokesman: "We will also have far more control over and protection of our intellectual property, which you don't have in China."

It was the state of Georgia's willingness to work with NCR to create an ecosystem that persuaded the company to move operations back from abroad and create jobs. "When we started the journey, *ecosystem* was the word we used," says Dorsman, who spent most of his career in the Midwest but moved to New York to be in better contact with large banks, retailers, and travel agencies. U.S. customers can easily visit the innovation center and other parts of NCR—product development, operations, customer training, parts, and logistics and services—because they are now all in the Atlanta area. The state helped NCR find or establish local suppliers to its plant, and the Georgia state university system has worked with NCR to come up with an executive development program for NCR's top management. "We have an interesting collection of resources in this ecosystem," says Dorsman.

It took less than six months for NCR to take the former Panasonic battery factory, gut it, and refurbish it to start operations in October 2009. Meanwhile, the state organized a job fair and 2,200 people lined up at the front door of the plant, the line extending down the street for four blocks, to apply for the initial 120 jobs. "The turnout was phenomenal, and that was instigated by Quick Start," Dorsman says. Quick Start is the state's technical college system that provides customized training to workforces in many different industries.

After hiring an initial batch of workers, the next key was going to be training them, and Quick Start also was involved in that. The company wanted to model the Georgia plant on how it was making ATMs in Budapest, Hungary. On a Friday, Dorsman was discussing the idea with Quick Start representatives on a conference call. "When would you like our crew to go to Budapest?" a state official asked.

"How about Monday?" Dorsman recalls asking. "And they did have a crew on the plane going to Budapest on Monday and spent quite a bit of time filming all the assembly. That was part of the training program we implemented. The state really had their act together."

The decisions that big businesses make have profound impact on people's lives—who has jobs, whose families can afford education, whose families can afford a decent home, whose families have health care, and who can enjoy a measure of overall economic security. Consider the case of Latonya Durham, who was hired at the NCR plant last summer. Even in small-town Georgia, she has felt the crosswinds of the global economy.

Durham, thirty-three, was born and bred in Junction City, Georgia (population 179), and is the single mother of two daughters. A high school graduate, she was working at a Cessna factory in early 2009 assembling small parts for aircraft, such as wing flaps. But the sales of Cessna's aircraft were in sharp decline because of the recession and higher fuel costs. "Cessna took a downturn because of the economy and they were forced to lay off some people, including me," she says, sitting at the desk of her supervisor in the Columbus plant, about twenty-five minutes by car from Junction City.[8]

Cessna decided to move some functions back to its headquarters in Wichita, Kansas, but much of the production would be shifted to Mexico. So before laying her off, along with hundreds of others, Cessna brought in the Mexican workers who would be doing their jobs and asked the American workers to train them. It was a moment of insight for Durham about how much different people in the world are paid for doing essentially the same thing. "We asked the Mexican guys, 'How much are y'all getting paid?'" she recalls. "They said $10 a day. To them, that was a lot of money. But to us, it wasn't."

She was out of a job on June 18, a date she remembers vividly because of the threat it posed to her family, including health benefits. "There are a lot of people who don't have those benefits," Durham says.

She took keen interest when she saw an ad in the newspaper for the NCR job fair, to be held one Saturday morning. "A couple of us got up and stood in line," she says. "We got there at five a.m. and the line was out of the parking lot."

Durham was one of the lucky ones. "My skills from previous jobs helped me get in the door," she explains. "I was hired within the first seventeen people." She started on July 27 and never applied for unemployment pay. The NCR job pays $11 an hour, slightly below what she was making at Cessna, but it includes health insurance.

After getting hired, the next step was training. Quick Start set up a monthlong course in a nearby building. She got paid during the training, which was provided free of charge. The first week was classroom work involving ergonomics and safety, but then in the following weeks the state brought in actual equipment of a sort being used in the plant and organized it into different workstations, much as the assembly line is set up at the plant. "I had to get new skills," she explains. "I had to learn how to take apart an ATM machine and rebuild it. I had to learn how to do the core box, which is the brains of the ATM."

NCR instructors arrived from Dundee, Scotland, to help in the training, which created linguistic confusion because of the different accents. "At first, it was a little shaky because of the language barrier," Durham recalls with a smile. "We couldn't understand them and they couldn't understand us. They said we talked too fast. We had to read lips."

They managed to overcome those barriers, and Durham is

aware that she has benefited from a high-level corporate decision to backshore production from China and other parts of
the world. "Coming back to America is a good thing because a
lot of people are unemployed and are searching for work," she
says. "It cuts down on the unemployment rate and helps to get
the economy started again. You're making money in America
and you're putting that money back in here. That's different
than if you do it in China."

It would be a mistake to conclude that large companies such as
NCR will ever move all their manufacturing back to the United
States. They will continue to scour the globe for other places
where they can create similar world-class ecosystems. In India,
China, Eastern Europe, and Brazil, NCR has built innovation
centers, co-located with its manufacturing operations, within
easy proximity of customers and suppliers. "That's our model,"
Dorsman explains. "That's what brings it together. What we're
doing is delivering comprehensive solutions including hardware,
software, and service. When we do it, we try to involve a government, a university, and suppliers. I would say our approach
is similar in these different places. It gets you into the ecosystem
and the region and allows you to be successful."

So American states and regions are competing with other ecosystems around the world to win investments from major companies that possess hundreds of billions of dollars in available
capital. U.S. states and regions can lure back sophisticated
products aimed at the American market if they create the right
climate for innovation. If a company feels that its long-term ability to serve customers and to innovate is enhanced by expanding
its presence in one of these U.S. ecosystems, it will happen. "I
do believe this will happen for products where innovation is
fundamental," says Dorsman.

The making of commoditized staples such as shoes, clothing,
and consumer electronics will mostly remain in Asia. "We're
not making 10 million cell phones a year that all look the same,"

Dorsman explains. "There is a lot of high variability and feature mix. If you're making cell phones overseas and shipping them in, that's a very different development and manufacturing model."

Backshoring will be more prevalent at the high end of the technology spectrum, in industries such as telecommunications and health care that are sensitive to quality and fast product cycles, or in cases in which companies feel they can profit from getting feedback from U.S. customers. As Georgia found, luring jobs home ultimately hinges on helping corporations achieve their goals of satisfying customers and making a profit while doing it.

★ ★ ★

NINE

The Race for the Right Skills
Cleveland Retrains Displaced Workers

JAMES LAMBERT WAS BORN and bred on the west side of Cleveland in a working-class family. For generations, his family worked at industrial jobs that did not require a college education, and these provided a good life. Confident of continued employment, his grandparents used to say, "If you do your job well, you have a job."[1]

But the first wave of dislocation hit Cleveland, and the rest of the American industrial economy, in the early 1980s. "Everybody got kicked in the pants," Lambert says—including his mother and father, both of whom were laid off.

Not able to finish high school, Lambert joined the military and earned a General Educational Development (GED) degree, or high school equivalency degree, before coming back to Cleveland and starting a series of factory jobs. In 1989, he went to work for a division of Gordon's Seafood, making the batter that McDonald's and Red Lobster restaurants use to prepare chicken and seafood. "It was pretty much grunt work, dealing with 50-pound boxes and bags for eight hours a day," Lambert recalls. The company was making batter on an industrial scale.

As he got older, the job became less tenable. "It got to the point that the mind was willing but the body couldn't do it," he jokes. He tried his hand in the sales division, but "I realized I wasn't much of a salesman," he says. He had an aptitude for machines and had always been able to repair automobiles, for example, so he left Gordon's and found work in a machine shop. That lasted for about a year before he was laid off in February 2009 at age forty-six.

It was a difficult economic period, coming at the depth of the country's worst postwar recession, and Lambert pounded the pavement for a couple of months and sent out many résumés before he realized that there was no work for him. He decided that he needed a higher set of skills.

He started checking into retraining programs at companies such as the Kaplan Career Institute. He thought they were expensive, but more important, these private schools told him that he would have to attend classes for a full year before he could obtain certificates showing he had received advanced training. Unemployment checks were coming in, but they would not last a full year and the family could not wait that long. Lambert's wife had a job at Macy's, selling clothing on the floor, "but she don't make much money," he says. They had two children.

At a job fair, Lambert saw a booth set up by Cuyahoga Community College (known as Tri-C) to promote its retraining programs. "The gentleman from Tri-C offered the exact same thing as the diploma mill schools did for roughly a quarter to a third of the cost," he explains. And instead of taking twelve months, Tri-C offered two accelerated quarters in advanced machining, which would take six months. He signed up.

Lambert had never taken algebra or trigonometry, but the Tri-C instructors were able to teach that math to Lambert because they demonstrated that it was necessary to operate advanced machines. He learned AutoCAD software, which allows the machine operator to take the dimensions of a part and instruct a machine how to make the part. Lambert also got his Tri-C certificate in computerized numerical controls.

With his last day of school scheduled for February 11, 2010, Lambert posted his résumé on Monster.com two days before that. Within a week, he received a phone call from a job recruiter who was looking for advanced machine operators for

DuPont Vespel, a subsidiary of DuPont that made precise parts for jet engines for Pratt & Whitney. Pratt, a unit of United Technologies, sold its engines to the U.S. military for single-engine jets.

The job, paying $16 an hour, was located in Valley View, a nearby suburb of Cleveland. Lambert was on the job by early March. It's a demanding job, partly because Lambert is on the overnight shift but also because the parts for single-engine jets have to be so carefully made. "The precision has to be there," he explains. "The tolerances I usually have to hold are five ten-thousands of an inch." That is smaller than a human hair. "I can basically take a human hair and split it three or four times" to get down to the scale of precision that the parts demand. He does it all on a manual machine.

He feels the money is good. "This is the most money I have ever made it in my life," says Lambert, now forty-seven. "I know even though I had twenty years of manufacturing experience, it was the courses at Tri-C that got me where I am today. If the program wasn't there, I would have been out of luck." He's getting a fair amount of overtime, which sweetens his paycheck. Within a year he will move to $18 an hour and start receiving full benefits.

He does not think he could have made the transition successfully at one of the private training schools. "Their thing is yeah, you get an education, but they're there to make money," Lambert says. "I didn't get that feeling from Tri-C. They don't treat it as a business. They treat it as a school. That program saved my family."

He feels he will enjoy solid job prospects for years to come and has some inkling of how he fits into broader global trends. "It's a proven fact—we're falling behind the rest of the world," he says. "The manufacturing base is gone basically. For fifteen or twenty years, you've had people not wanting to go into machining because the jobs weren't there. Now that the older machinists are retiring, there's nobody to replace them."

Lambert's story is hardly unique in a place such as Cleveland. Many workers with similar backgrounds tell stories about endless job churn. They are laid off and after a period of time are able to find new jobs, perhaps paying less than their old jobs. And then after eighteen months or two years, those jobs also come to an end. In this environment, human resources are "disposable," one complains bitterly. The ability of these workers to achieve steadily escalating incomes as their families need educational and medical support is sharply constrained. Their lives often take the additional hit of not having medical insurance when a loved one is stricken with cancer or another debilitating disease, when housing values plunge, or some combination thereof. It can quickly become the American Dream in reverse. "Many of the jobs lost during the recession are not coming back. Period," wrote the *New York Times*.[2] It said that for millions of workers, "the occupations they worked in, and the skills they currently possess, are never coming back in style."

The *Wall Street Journal* agreed that many of the jobs created by the booms in the housing and credit markets during the bubble years have been permanently erased.[3] Jobs in construction, for example, were ideal for men without college educations. But that sector was slammed particularly hard, accounting for more than a fifth of the jobs lost since the recession began. Companies in many industries cut jobs no longer as critical as they once were because of advances in information technology.

This permanent, brutal shift in the job market helps explain why many displaced workers have turned to the retraining program at Tri-C and others under way at the nation's twelve hundred community colleges.[4] The debate about how to retrain workers, mainly in their forties and fifties, who have been displaced is critical to the future of the whole economy. If the United States cannot develop the engineers, technicians, and other skilled workers to support the genomics, advanced robotics, or lithium-ion battery industries, the companies seeking to make those products will have little choice but to either import non-Americans or else go offshore.

Of course, the skills gap in the American workforce is a broad educational challenge that includes encouraging young people to strive for better educations in fields that are relevant to the needs of business. But young people still have time; the more crucial challenge may be the one facing people in their forties and fifties. They are at risk of being destroyed economically at the very moment that their families turn to them for support.

These people have traditionally faced a huge vacuum. By and large, companies have been skittish about spending heavily on retraining programs because they are an expensive proposition with limited returns; in fact, the smartest workers who get the most out of the training can parlay it into higher-paying jobs at competing enterprises. Four-year universities, for their part, have tenured professors and a more rigid curriculum, and philosophically are less inclined to allow employers to shape the agenda of what happens in the classroom.

Federal and state agencies have been disappointingly ineffective. As early as 1962, when John F. Kennedy was president, a program known as Trade Adjustment Assistance was put in place to help workers who lost their jobs as a result of increased imports. But that program had to make do with minimal budgets most years, and did not have a great impact. During the 1990s, the debate over the North American Free Trade Agreement (which critics such as H. Ross Perot said in 1992 would create a "giant sucking sound" of jobs headed to Mexico)[5] included calls by labor advocates for better worker retraining efforts. But again, little progress was made. One reason is that many of the key functions within the employment and retraining operations of the federal departments of Labor and Education have been starved of funding or been a repository for largely ineffective political appointees. The Workforce Investment Act, passed in 1998, did not fundamentally alter the pattern of failure.

Private trade schools and other retraining programs, meanwhile, sometimes make big promises about employment prospects and then cannot deliver. Or else, as Lambert found, they charge too much money and take too long. Overall, it is a maddeningly dense thicket of organizations that have not delivered results for workers who face marginalization or even elimination from the workforce. Becoming a greeter in a Walmart or stocking the shelves in a Home Depot cannot help most former industrial workers adequately support their families.

This vacuum is what has created an opening for community colleges. The Tri-C program's funding comes from federal, state, and local governments as well as private foundations. Some fifty-five thousand students are enrolled in its programs each year, including the retraining programs. President Obama gave a big boost to these programs in July 2009 when he traveled to Macomb Community College in hard-hit Warren, Michigan, and proposed $12 billion in new federal funding for community colleges over the next decade.[6] That amount was later trimmed to $2 billion, but still the role of community colleges seems to be advancing.

In the best cases, community college leaders have relationships with local business leaders and government officials and possess the institutional flexibility to build relationships, to find convergences of interest, as part of a regional ecosystem. The Tri-C program, which is recognized as one of the ten best among community colleges, has a wide range of relationships with local employers. The prestigious Cleveland Clinic medical system works with the school to teach job seekers the ins and outs of the medical and health care fields. And former autoworkers are learning about manufacturing processes in solar energy plants producing photovoltaic cells. "If you look at clean renewable energy, the folks who used to make auto parts can learn how to make wind turbines," says Dr. Craig Follins, executive vice president of Tri-C's workforce and economic development division. "What you're doing is morphing from manufacturing cars to newer advanced industries."[7]

In a similar vein, Tri-C's joint effort with Ford Motor Company drives a curriculum that teaches skills needed at the automaker's Brook Park, Ohio, plant, which has started making a more energy-efficient engine called the EcoBoost. The whole point of this type of training is to prevent workers from being laid off in the first place.

Critics argue that community colleges are training people for more environmentally oriented jobs than currently exist, which is why it's important for the training programs to be diversified. Consider the case of Ben Venue, a maker of freeze-dried and injectable pharmaceutical products, which employed twelve hundred people in the Cleveland area as of late 2009 and was looking for at least another one hundred. The Bedford, Ohio–based manufacturer is one of the largest employers in the fledgling biotechnology and pharmaceutical corridor that industrial development authorities are trying to establish between Cleveland and Pittsburgh.

Considering severe job losses in Ohio, it would seem that Ben Venue's search for workers would have been a relatively easy task. But it was not. Virtually none of the workers displaced from the auto, plastics, tire, or steel industries had the skills required to make drugs in sterile environments that meet FDA guidelines.

So Ben Venue process control manager Phil Mills, a Briton, turned to Tri-C to develop a 160-hour course on pharmaceutical manufacturing for people interested in jobs at Ben Venue or other local drug companies. Mills and a team of five Ben Venue employees advised Tri-C on what kind of equipment to buy for the courses—devices and apparel similar to those used in the company's factories.

Making things in an aseptic, or clean, environment is a whole different arena from what most workers are used to. "People have to understand the rules for gowning themselves," Mills explains. "When you go into a clean room, you have to ensure that none of particles from your body can come into the atmosphere."[8] They also have to make sure that nothing that is potentially hazardous from inside the clean room escapes into the outside world. The class at Tri-C puts students through the process of gowning themselves properly. "Then we test these people afterward to make sure they aren't contaminated," he says. It may seem simple, but it has to be done correctly every time.

The classes were first offered in mid-2008. "We're trying to create a labor pool with some initial knowledge of what the pharmaceutical industry is all about," says Mills, who also teaches some of the courses. Ben Venue has just hired its first graduate from the program.

Tri-C is considered particularly effective because it has either formal or informal committees of employers, such as the one from Ben Venue, that help guide the curriculum for each retraining program, ensuring that the classes are customized to provide skill sets that companies are actually looking for. "Community colleges are going to be the retraining providers for most of the folks who have been displaced," says Follins. "We're nimble. We're malleable. We're located close to where most Americans live."

Follins, fifty-two, has pursued an interesting path to arrive in this position. He was raised in the tough Bushwick section of Brooklyn, New York, and used to play stickball in the streets. He had a single parent in the home, his mother, who tried to keep Follins and his siblings out of trouble and focused on education. He was not able to finish high school. Instead he joined the military and got a GED there, as Lambert did.

He spent ten years in workforce development and economic development positions in Houston, Texas, helping chicken factories and ice cream factories, among others, find and train the right workers. Follins next moved to Victoria, Texas, a rural community two hours southwest of Houston, and continued working to train people. In Victoria, six big petrochemical companies including Dow Chemical and Formosa Plastics employ a total of fifteen thousand employees. Follins went on to get a PhD in educational administration with a focus on community college leadership from the University of Texas at Austin in 2004.

Follins has thus worked his way up the ladder of life and helped thousands of others try to do the same thing. That has equipped him with a vision of the importance of education and the role that the public sector plays in developing human capital. He arrived in Cleveland in August 2007 and, although he didn't create the Tri-C retraining program, he has expanded it.

Why hasn't the United States done a better job redeploying people? "The urgency wasn't there," is how Follins explains it. But the reality of sustained global competition is becoming clearer to more people. "Global competition is coming from Russia and China and India and Singapore," he says. "So how do we prepare folks? The future is less about traditional manufacturing skills and more about critical thinking skills and advanced manufacturing in a knowledge-based economy."

That's a tough message for people who were comfortable with the idea of getting a high school diploma, joining a union, and enjoying a good middle-class life. In northern Ohio, that was the way it was for hundreds of thousands of workers for several generations. "Traditional manufacturing is the poster child for that paradigm," Follins says. "Now we've found that doesn't work. Now many of those people have to go back to school to get a whole new education."

Many of these workers get frustrated when they approach local workforce boards, which is where much federal money flows, because those offices are rarely equipped to offer retraining. They frequently refer displaced workers to other programs, such as the privately run vocational schools or occupational training centers. The National Skills Coalition, a grouping of more than fourteen hundred organizations in twenty-five states, is trying to improve federal retraining efforts at the local level but points to numerous bureaucratic barriers, such as rules that require workforce boards to offer certain kinds of training in a prescribed order, regardless of a worker's actual needs. "There needs to be a way of delivering the services quicker," says Follins. "If I am a General Motors worker and I'm laid off, I should be able to walk into a community college and say, 'I need retraining.'"

Of great significance is the fact that Follins concentrates on specific industrial clusters to offer training and retraining. One new focus is smart energy grids, and Tri-C just received a grant from the Department of Energy to train two hundred Cleveland Public Power employees how to shift gears from the old electricity distribution-generating model to a new one. Former line workers and cable splicers will learn how to build a smart grid in northern Ohio. The curriculum that Tri-C develops will be shared with other community colleges.

Transportation is another cluster. Follins in 2008 created a regional transportation institute that includes classes in commercial trucking, diesel engines, logistics, warehousing, and related fields. More than a hundred students have graduated and taken jobs paying from $27,000 to $50,000 a year. Still another is electronic health records, which is a major federal priority. Tri-C is the lead college in a five-state consortium to develop training courses to help workers learn how to manage these electronic records and systems. Follins argues that these patterns of cooperation among states and community colleges are essential. "By leveraging your resources you can affect more people," he says. "You can't do everything by yourself."

Critics might argue that the federal government is wasting taxpayer money by supporting training and retraining programs that ought to be left to the private sector, but Follins disagrees. "That's not the federal government's money," he argues. "That's our tax money coming back to us. It's not coming from a big brother. We're investing in our own success. We are paying for our own programs. The federal government is just a broker that collects the money and redistributes the funds. Historically, in hard times, the federal government has always stepped in and been the arbiter, moving things forward."

The fact that the money is concentrated on specific industries, or clusters, suggests that the money is not being spent in an unfocused way. "The federal government says we need to grow clusters, and community colleges need to develop programs to feed those," he says. "You just don't grow a company. You grow the cluster. It makes sense to purposefully feed the cluster."

Of course, Follins couldn't manage a successful program unless he was able to draw others into a shared vision, such as John Gajewski, a former executive at General Electric, Emerson Electric, and Berkshire Hathaway. Follins concentrates more on managing relationships with outside governmental and business organizations, while executive directors such as Gajewski concentrate on the classroom.

Gajewski came out of retirement two years ago to run Tri-C's training for advanced manufacturing, biosciences, engineering, and skilled trades. Now fifty-eight, the Milwaukee native has exactly the right kind of background: at GE, for example, he held management positions in three divisions, Medical Systems, Appliances, and Aerospace, and went through the company's highly regarded training program for executives at Crotonville, New York.

He became acutely aware of the mismatch of skills in the American workforce about ten years ago when, as part of his job at the time, he was in charge of adding a hundred workers to his company's operations to increase a factory's production. But he had to review five hundred applications to find the right hundred people. That experience demonstrated to him what he calls "the shortfalls in our training and educational systems."[9]

In Cleveland, he started doing volunteer work on the side at a nonprofit called Jobs Partnership Cleveland, which concentrated on both unemployed and underemployed individuals. He retired from full-time work, but his interest in workforce issues persisted and he discovered the teaching opportunity at Tri-C. "That opportunity to bridge the gap between education and training and business is what persuaded me to leave retirement," he says.

Most of his instructors, it turns out, are engineers or technical people in their fifties or sixties who are enjoying a second career rather than leaving the workforce entirely. "As we baby boomers move from our primary careers, we can continue to contribute to the regions that we live in by entering into a secondary career. In my case, it's the workforce."

He knows exactly what hard skills his students need because of Tri-C's industrial advisory councils. Companies represented on those councils, such as Ben Venue and Ford, are very specific about the kinds of workers they want. As Lambert found, math skills are one key. But the math needs to be taught in the right way. "If we told our students we are going to do trigonometry now, there would be a pullback reaction," Gajewski explains. "But by building trigonometry into blueprint reading and into projects that are done on our machinery, our students are learning higher-level math in a contextual manner. They can apply it to problems that they are trying to solve."

Gajewski says workers need to gain more than just technical skills, however. "The technical content is fairly straightforward— it's the people skills and the employability skills that take a little bit of creativity, because those skills are not scientific," he says. Many workers coming out of an older industrial setting, he notes, don't understand the importance of teamwork and communications in newer, more flexible manufacturing systems, so his instructors teach groups of workers how to interact on a project. They assemble two or three people to work as a team to, for example, produce a part they designed. "You can lecture on the need for teamwork, but it only works if they buy into it and accept it," he says.

Another piece that's missing from many retraining programs, Gajewski says, is counseling to help the displaced deal with the raw emotions caused by what has happened to them. "What we need to work through with them is any kind of resentment or anxiety they have in making a career change," he explains. "A laid-off worker has had some damage done to their psyche and their self-esteem. We need to do some work on that."

Again, the burning question is why it has taken this long to get serious about retraining in the United States. "Our economy has been very good for so long," he says. "We were successful, and success bred complacency. We didn't fully recognize international competition, globalization, and the impact it might have on our businesses."

But now companies deep in the Midwest are exposed to the full brunt of global competition and have no choice but to drive up the technology ladder. "What companies are doing to be globally competitive both from the standpoint of productivity and quality is that they are using more automated and sophisticated equipment and computer-integrated manufacturing," he adds. "The worker of today and tomorrow needs to be more technically competent and computer literate, and that's the type of training we are doing."

Add it all up and it does seem that community colleges such as Tri-C have critical advantages—direct connections with employers, accredited technical training that is combined with counseling for those who want it, and knowledgeable faculty. "Long considered the backwater of higher education, community colleges have found themselves at the vanguard of training the U.S. work force as laid-off employees clamor for new opportunities," the *Wall Street Journal* wrote.[10]

No one would argue that the programs being offered by community colleges are big enough and numerous enough to retrain all the workers who have been displaced. But they are clearly demonstrating how federal, state, and local governments can work with employers and community colleges to create an educational ecosystem that fills a major gap in how America trains and retrains its people.

This is a critical national challenge—if there are to be people to work in the new industries that are being created, if there are to be people who can build new energy systems, if there are to be people who understand how to export and create winning international strategies, the United States must improve its workforce.

Obviously, creating a successful retraining ecosystem is very different from creating a technology hotspot, but there are commonalities. It can be created and does not have to happen by accident. Key nonpolitical professionals need to be in the right positions and must be motivated to strive toward a higher good. Different institutions—federal and state governments, business leaders, and community colleges—have to identify and exploit mutual opportunities. There must be alignment. And these players, from disparate backgrounds, must understand their roles. Among other things, that means they must understand that the federal government plays an important role in seeding the clouds but cannot control or dictate the final outcomes.

Other nations are far ahead of the United States in consciously shaping the skills of their workforces, and those programs tend to be centralized and mandated by their national governments. The more distributed and decentralized American educational model at the grassroots level still has huge power, however, if properly deployed. Tri-C is powerful evidence of that.

PART III

★ ★ ★

THE BLUEPRINT FOR
REAL RECOVERY

TEN

Building Ecosystems at the State and Local Levels

R ATHER THAN BUILDING CASINOS or big-box retailers, the creation or expansion of a technology cluster is the most sustainable way of responding to global competition and mitigating the vagaries of business cycle gyrations. It also is a more efficient wealth generator on a national scale because clusters have a high export ratio, meaning that they are making money in the world outside the United States. Clusters allow Americans to create world-class advantages that cannot be imitated quickly by others. This is the kind of wealth that can endure, and it is how new ideas come to dominate their niches internationally. This is how Americans take their highly innovative ideas and translate them into industries, helping to build or rebuild the industrial "commons" that have eroded over the years. Japan, China, and virtually every other advanced nation in the world understand these benefits, which is why they target these activities and why many have created their own cluster strategies.

There are hundreds of clusters in the United States, but the phenomenon is not well understood. In the old days, it was easy to associate cars with Detroit, steel with Pittsburgh, tires with Akron, glass with Toledo, and insurance with Hartford. Those were clusters. Today, aside from well-known spots such as Silicon Valley, there is the state of Maine's cluster for the manufacturing of boats; Louisville, Kentucky's transportation and logistics hot spot; and Boise, Idaho's semiconductor industry, which is the result of potato baron J. R. Simplot's early investment in Micron Technology. "Centuries of evidence indicate that the geographic clustering of organizations in a sector significantly facilitates innovation and creativity, productivity, access to essential key inputs such as skilled labor and materials, and improved operating costs," said a study by the Metropolitan Policy Program of the Brookings Institution in 2008.[1]

These characteristics have been amply displayed in the case studies in this book, but it is helpful to understand Brookings' analytical framework. "Industry clusters develop through the attractions of geographic proximity—firms find that geographic concentration of similar, related, complementary, and supporting organizations offers a wide array of benefits," it added. "Clusters promote knowledge-sharing ('spillovers') and innovations in products and in technical and business processes by providing thick networks of formal and informal relationships across organizations." This last phrase is particularly valuable—"thick networks of formal and informal relationships across organizations."

How are clusters created? The IC^2 Institute in Austin argues that that city's technology explosion was the result of a "road map" that its founder, George Kozmetsky, consciously helped to create. But most clusters do not appear to be planned, says Andrew Reamer, a fellow at Brookings and one of the coauthors of the institute's study. "It's very difficult to create a cluster," Reamer explains. "Clusters tend to happen by accident. The factors that bring clusters into being are difficult for a government to control. It can be done. But the more important role for governments are to enhance the competitiveness of existing and emerging clusters."[2]

As *BusinessWeek* described the role of government in 1992 in its "Hot Spots" cover story: "While different levels of government can build infrastructure, fund universities, and provide seed capital, the real key lies with local coalitions of business leaders and educators. Rather than relying on a centralized bureaucracy akin to Japan's Ministry of International Trade &

Industry, the American approach works best when it is local and decentralized."[3]

The new contribution to the debate in recent years has been the growing acceptance of the term *ecosystem* to describe the pattern of interactions among multiple players in the private sector, government, and education. I prefer the term *ecosystem* to another word, *infrastructure*, because the biological term implies that a cluster has a life of its own, which it does. There are many different kinds of interactions, and they are dependent on personalities and politics. In contrast, the word *infrastructure* implies something that is static and fixed.

Sometimes multiple ecosystems can exist in a single well-developed cluster. North Carolina, for example, has ecosystems that allow the commercialization of technology, but also ones that encourage exports and train workers. Austin is strong on technology commercialization, energy, and training but does not have the same export emphasis that Silicon Valley has. Other ecosystems, such as NCR's ATM operations in Georgia and Tri-C's training and retraining efforts in Cleveland, can exist outside of a technology cluster. There are at least four overlapping kinds of ecosystems, and the next sections explore them.

TECHNOLOGY COMMERCIALIZATION ECOSYSTEMS

IDEA FACTORIES ARE AT THE HEART of this ecosystem. They can be a university, a government weapons lab such as Sandia or Lawrence Livermore, or an institute such as the Mayo Clinic or Scripps Research Institute. The idea factory also can be a large company, such as Disney in Orlando, that seeds talent into start-up companies such as IDEAS. Technology and ideas are diffused in many ways; sometimes they move when people move.

An important characteristic of this ecosystem is that different scientific and academic disciplines are located in close proximity—computer people have regular contact with genetic researchers and robotic specialists bump into software gurus in the hall, for example. These people, ideally, are encouraged to interact with each other on a sustained basis across traditional industry or professional lines, both officially and unofficially. This melting pot, or crossroads, effect is crucial.

So too is the cultural dimension. Knowledge-based innovation rarely occurs in a monocultural context. I have never visited a node of wealth-creating activity in the United States without finding people who are transplants from elsewhere in the country and from around the world. These people have been attracted to a location not only by its quality of life but also by the chance to pursue their dreams. Because of those factors, once sleepy towns such as Orlando and Austin and San Diego are now international crossroads.

In successful ecosystems, idea factories have policies that favor the movement of ideas outside their walls. Universities must have enlightened policies to allow ideas they own to be commercialized and to allow professors and students time to try to do it. "Some universities are better than others," says Garry Neil of Johnson & Johnson. "MIT is very good at it. It spends a lot of time thinking about how to make the process work better on the intellectual property side and has good industry liaison programs. Some smaller universities are not that well staffed or don't have the same level of commitment to it." And for a weapons lab run by the Department of Energy, the key is the Cooperative Research and Development Agreements (CRADAs) that business-minded people negotiate to obtain access to advanced technologies.

The entrepreneurs often need incubators or halfway houses to take the first step out of the idea factory. Once in the incubator, they need a precise mix of incentives. Entrepreneurs who show progress and have a promising idea need to be encouraged to move forward, both in terms of mentoring and financial support, including the possibility of grants. If grants are made, however, the danger is that entrepreneurs will have an incentive just to keep taking free money and not make tough decisions about how to commercialize their ideas. Some incubators are not in a hurry for inventors to commercialize their ideas and move out because they have an incentive in continuing to receive rent payments. Their primary interest is in earning money from real estate, not creating commercial enterprises. Achieving just the right balance so that innovators have incentives to commercialize and incubators have incentives to help make that happen requires real wisdom.

As an idea evolves, networks of angel investors may be better at providing the initial seed capital than most venture capital firms. The latter firms tend not to want to play in such risky waters, and commercial banks are nowhere to be seen if the prospect of commercialization could be years away, on the other side of the valley of death. "You can't have the research sitting there in the lab without the individual wealth available to commercialize the ideas," as John Sibley Butler from IC^2 in Austin says. Thus a region's wealthy individuals have a clear leadership role to play.

Government money also can be key in the early stages: A123's Yet-Ming Chiang received an early $100,000 grant from the Small Business Administration and the Department of Energy that helped him develop his battery idea, for example, and the University of Central Florida is adept at winning Small Business Innovation Research grants. Funding from NSF and NIH is often critical; corporate research and contract research also can play a role.

But most of the money needed to successfully commercialize an idea ultimately comes from private sector investors. In the early stages, whether it is from angel investors or venture capitalists, entrepreneurs need patient money, meaning funds from individuals or firms that are not seeking exit strategies within a year or eighteen months, and also smart money, meaning funds that are administered by CEOs who have run businesses before. In short, the money has to be the right kind of money; if venture capitalists lend money and want double-digit rates of return in short order, the new business may be doomed.

It's clear that the private sector is the ultimate arbiter in a system in which money flows to, say, ten ideas. One entrepreneur hits a home run, three will hit singles, and the rest may strike out. Failure is actually important. The weak must fail and fail quickly so that resources can be concentrated on the best ideas with the best managements and therefore the best chances of successful commercialization.

Why is it that some regions have vibrant venture capital communities and others don't? "It's not random," says San Diego's Ivor Royston. A key factor investors look for is universities and research institutes that allow ideas to move beyond their walls and encourage researchers to explore them. "Wherever you have active participation by venture capitalists, it is connected to a high degree of entrepreneurship," Royston argues. "Institutes have to be very supportive of entrepreneurship and risk taking. Universities have to have the right technology transfer policies and not be too stringent on faculty getting involved in commercialization. You need the institutions to tell their people, 'If you have a good idea, go talk to the venture capitalists.' Others that didn't do that have lagged behind."

So state and regional leaders eager to attract the attention of venture capitalists from other cities or to develop an indigenous venture capital community have a tool they can use—engaging with leaders of universities, institutes, and labs to persuade them to adopt polices encouraging the diffusion of their technology.

Venture capitalists also are attracted to quality of management, another decisive factor that can be developed. The professors or entrepreneurs who have a fascination for a particular technology need to bring in MBAs and people with solid business experience. A hefty percentage of scientists who launch ideas recruit professional CEOs, who often put the companies through a wrenching refocusing, as Dave Vieau did with A123 Systems in Boston and Eric Close did with RedZone in Pittsburgh. One set of people may be involved in creating the ideas, but a very different mix of people needs to be involved in commercializing them. That's one gap in Pittsburgh's and North Carolina's ecosystems. There is an abundance of professors and young PhDs with hot ideas, but a shortage of chief executive officers who can take those ideas and scale them. In the interest of attracting venture capitalists, state and local leaders should ensure that their business schools keep pace with their research universities and institutes. Programs to encourage scientists to mingle with business leaders can be highly effective, as MIT has found.

Another key element of a technology ecosystem is the presence of large, established companies that often invest in the start-ups, license their technology, or sit on their boards. General Electric has played that role for A123; companies such as Boeing, Caterpillar, Intel, Procter & Gamble, and IBM are other major players in seeking to identify and network with the best minds in key universities. Major pharmaceutical companies from around the world are key players in San Diego's biotech cluster.

One role that the CEOs and senior executives of larger firms can play is that of mentoring less experienced leaders of small companies. No textbook can fully prepare an emerging CEO to truly make it; the body of knowledge about how to do that resides principally with those who have done it. That's why mentoring programs or councils can be so crucial. Boston, Silicon Valley, Research Triangle Park, and Austin have clear advantages over younger clusters because they have created several generations of companies and have smoothly oiled mechanisms for entrepreneurs to connect with seasoned financiers, managers, and others.

It seems that a community or region needs a stage-gate process, like those Corning, IBM, and other major companies have internally, to discuss their ecosystem and its gaps. The lack of an agreed-upon vocabulary can be a handicap for many states and regions. Stage 1 could be considered the research itself inside the idea factory. Getting the right technology transfer policies in place is the prerequisite for the idea to make it to Stage 2, meaning an incubator or halfway house where it can be developed into a commercially viable proposition. This is where the management team becomes engaged and some angel investing takes place. Then by Stage 3, more business-minded leaders have to be introduced into the mix, possibly including a CEO. More capital is raised. Stage 4 could be considered a full concentration on the market, not just the technology. The technology becomes a profitable business in Stage 5 and scales up.

If an ecosystem were mapped out in this way, regional leaders could identify the gaps and seek to plug in the holes. For this value chain to function successfully, different institutions have to be involved and they have to cooperate. They must work to advance their own interests as part of a shared vision.

ENERGY ECOSYSTEMS

OTHER TYPES OF ECOSYSTEMS share many of the characteristics described above, but with a twist. I would argue that a slightly different kind of ecosystem is necessary to tackle complex energy challenges because the United States needs new models to attack its dependence on imported energy and on fossil fuels. Merely continuing current institutional alignments, which provide incentives to utilities to defend existing energy patterns relying on large-scale power production and distribution of power across hundreds of miles of transmission lines, almost certainly will not suffice.

In Austin, environmentalists and community activists concerned about energy costs were drawn into a coalition with a utility company, the city council, the chamber of commerce, and the University of Texas and its incubator. Big companies such as Applied Materials saw clear business opportunities and contributed time and money. The Pecan Street Project had a leader, Brewster McCracken, who had been a politician but had established credibility for even-handedness and vision. The credibility of leadership is hugely important—leaders have to demonstrate that they are committed to an idea for the larger good, not just for self-enhancement.

McCracken was the facilitator, but ideas flowed from many

different directions. Building Austin's new energy ecosystem was not a simple flow of a single technology from an idea factory, but rather the building of a consensus. One end result may be the creation of businesses that can profit from an era of distributed renewable energy. Of course, this ecosystem exists as part of a larger, highly successful technology cluster, which in some ways created the conditions that allowed the Pecan Street Project to launch itself, but it is very different from a technology commercialization ecosystem.

EXPORT PROMOTION ECOSYSTEMS

INFORMATION AND EXPERTISE also need to flow to promote exports—knowledge about trade shows and export opportunities needs to flow from around the world into a region. The U.S. Department of Commerce and state export offices need to play a leading role in supplementing the role of the Internet in doing that. Technology councils, economic development agencies, trading companies, private export promotion companies, and other players also are involved, but the great risk is that little of the information they communicate is relevant and targeted. Another risk is that when a small company seeks advice about how to take advantage of the information, the local export promotion official simply does not know. It is beyond his or her expertise. The exporter is referred to someone else in a bureaucratic runaround.

So if this thicket of agencies cannot be streamlined, alliances need to be created among them to move quality information to the right recipients and to provide them with practical advice. Mentoring is particularly important to would-be exporters because there is so much to learn—how to adapt to different cultures, how to find and manage distributors, how to adapt one's product to different markets, how to manage a company that operates in multiple time zones, and the like.

The most glaring need, however, is providing the capital to would-be exporters so that they can take the risk of expanding production and shipping products to a foreign country. Commercial banks, hit by the freeze-up in financial markets, have retreated from this activity. The Department of Commerce, Small Business Administration, and Export-Import Bank are supposed to be cooperating with state and local export officials to create seamless, one-stop shopping for exporters needing this financial support, but it has been slow in coming. Strong local leadership can accelerate and facilitate that. Huge progress can be achieved in rationalizing and improving regional export promotion efforts.

WORKFORCE TRAINING AND RETRAINING ECOSYSTEMS

WHEN IT COMES TO TRAINING and retraining, localities also need institutional flexibility of a sort that Cleveland has displayed with Tri-C. Rather than different institutions remaining apart and safeguarding their parochial interests, they need to find an overlap of interests. Tri-C raises money from local, state, and federal governments, plus nonprofits and foundations. It has relations with the chamber of commerce and many universities and businesses. The alliances with businesses are key because they provide knowledge about what employers are truly looking for in terms of workers. As Tri-C's Craig Follins says, the community colleges should go about their training programs in a way that "feeds the cluster," or attempts to train and retrain people to do the jobs that community leaders envision creating. That is a critical insight. The responsibility for this ecosystem is once again fractured, but the system can be made to perform if the players find overlapping interests. They all win more by cooperating than by remaining isolated. Georgia's Quick Start is a slightly different example because it is an alliance of technical colleges, supported by the state, but it also has been quite effective.

• • •

The takeaway is that America's wide-open, often combative, and always argumentative society must cohere better in the face of competitors that have centralized state-driven technological and economic strategies. Americans should apply systematic thinking to that task and develop common vocabulary and common processes for understanding crucial economic functions, a realm where economists are largely absent.

There's no single magical formula. A state or locality does not necessarily have to have an institute, a technology council, a chamber of commerce, or an economic development agency. If there are too many of these organizations and they have overlapping charters, the end result can be complexity and dysfunctionality. In that case, consolidation and streamlining make a great deal of sense. IC^2 in Austin notes that the Texas Department of Commerce represents the consolidation of the Texas Economic Development Commission, the Texas World Trade Council, the Texas Enterprise Zone Board, the Technology Training Board, and other bodies.

Ultimately, the institutions themselves may be less important than the climate of cooperation that is created. Getting the relationships right between a mayor, chamber of commerce, local CEOs, and a university, say, is more important than the precise institutional framework. What's essential is a climate that allows ideas to emerge or be shared. That's why a stand-alone research park will not work—it lacks the "thick network" of relationships among players from different institutions.

There are other subtle cultural issues. A successful cluster needs facilitators who move information around and have personal connections built up over a period of years. I often can tell whether a community has a winning culture when I make my first requests for interviews. If I can find an agency or university or a chamber of commerce that can introduce me to many or most key players, chances are that community's decision-making processes are well-oiled. If I have to reach out individually to different players and they do not appear to speak to one another, chances are that the community is balkanized and divided. New Jersey's export ecosystem, for example, was clearly broken.

The management of these ecosystems—or what is generally called economic development work—should not be controlled by a governor or mayor. Governors and mayors, as political creatures, tend to stack key economic development positions with allies who don't have the necessary expertise. Agencies that depend too heavily on a state or local government for financial support also often find themselves scrambling to produce pay-offs in the short term, one year or two, to justify their funding. This has the effect of encouraging the development agencies to go for quick hits, such as luring in a factory relocation, rather than developing long-term policies, which are the only policies that work in nurturing economic growth. "We've had a swing-ing door for the past dozen years in Trenton," says a frustrated Maxine Ballen, executive director of the New Jersey Technology Council. "In my first ten years here, we had six governors. It cre-ated an inconsistency and a disruption in what would have been a series of well-executed actions. Each time a governor came in, they had to disrupt things and put their own mark on it. We've been handicapped by that." That's precisely what North Caro-lina has avoided by having consistent policies in place.

Agencies that are too dependent on the vagaries of politics find their funding gets cut at the first whiff of a budget crisis. The *Wall Street Journal* reported in May 2010 that many state governments seeking to close budget gaps were shutting down tax credit and incentive programs. "At a time when sharp drops in revenue are forcing state and local governments to lay off teachers, it makes a lot of sense to take a hard look at tax sub-sidies to business," Michael Mazerov, a senior fellow at the Center on Budget and Policy Priorities, was quoted as saying.[4] Others disagreed, saying it was shortsighted to curtail their in-vestment and employment attraction policies.

Duane Roth, CEO of San Diego's CONNECT nonprofit technology development agency, which has been widely studied by other cities, argues that development agencies should not be dependent on *any* single source for funding. "When people at those agencies tell me they might be able to obtain a large $2 million grant, I say, 'Don't take it,'" he explains. "You never want to be in that position" of having to seek approval from a dominant funding source for a particular decision. Roth says other explanations why his agency has been successful are that it insists on choosing former businesspeople as its CEO and lodges real decision-making power in that CEO. That is different from many agencies that appoint an executive director who must constantly seek the ratification of a board. The added virtue of appointing a businessperson to lead an agency, as opposed to a professional nonprofit person, is that he or she will bring a private-sector perspective to how wealth and jobs are created. Last, Roth argues that any development agency has to remain neutral and objective in its programs and for that reason should never invest in companies. That creates a financial motivation, which undermines the agency's credibility with other participants. "You have to maintain neutrality and be a trusted source by all the players," he advises.

An obvious corollary is that any form of corruption, nepotism, or patronage undermines confidence in the integrity of players attempting to create or improve an economic ecosystem. The decisions about which institutions and which companies receive public funds should be based on transparent criteria. Even a hint of backroom dealing can destroy any hope of building a vibrant ecosystem.

For all these reasons, the best ecosystems involve government agencies as partners but do not depend on them. Ideally, there is some coordination with federal priorities, but it should be done in a bottom-up way rather than merely accepting a top-down approach from Washington. If a region has a successful ecosystem of any variety, Washington should be asked for support but should not be in a position of control. Federal money can be crucial in generating research and some early financing, but at a certain point in the life cycle of a company or a project, the federal role is lessened. A state or city has to marshal different resources to focus on growing the idea. There's a natural endpoint to any direct government involvement: Once a company has commercialized a technology or created a successful export program, it no longer needs a helping hand. Participants should display a profound respect for the power of the market and the limits of government involvement.

There are no guarantees in any ecosystem. New Jersey once boasted a telecommunications cluster, but that collapsed after the sale of AT&T and Lucent to other companies. Even Silicon Valley faces a constant battle to prevent itself from being eclipsed or eroded. Austin has suffered from a decline in semiconductor sales and from plants moving offshore. Shortages of venture capital, management talent, and adequately trained labor are constant issues. In a capitalist system characterized by Schumpeter's "creative destruction," clusters have to constantly refresh and keep moving to the next level. The process never ends.

Questions for a State or Region

- What is your competitive advantage? What industries or ideas make you special?

- Do you have the right leadership in place in government, business, academia, and other civic institutions? Do they cooperate on some level? Do they share a common vision?

- What are the gaps in the ecosystems that you hope will create wealth?

ELEVEN

The Federal Government and Industrial Policy

D ATING BACK TO THE BIRTH of the nation, one of the most important debates in the land—and one of the most divisive—has been about the role of the federal government in the economy. In the twentieth century, Republican president Herbert Hoover did not believe the government had a responsibility to pull the country out of the Great Depression. But Franklin D. Roosevelt, a Democrat, took office in 1933 and swung the pendulum in the other direction, embarking on New Deal programs that built infrastructure and created jobs. It was only the economic buildup to support American forces in World War II, however, that ultimately pulled the economy out of the doldrums.

Steps that the government took in pursuit of broad national objectives have had major economic impact. The Manhattan Project was launched to develop an atomic bomb, which ended the war against Japan, but it also has created a nuclear power industry and a raft of technologies that have emerged from the national weapons labs. The Marshall Plan rebuilt the economies of Western Europe to stabilize them against Soviet Communism but also created huge markets for U.S. companies. Then after the Soviet Union surprised American leaders by putting Sputnik into orbit, the government responded by creating NASA and the Advanced Research Projects Agency (ARPA, predecessor to the current DARPA), both in 1957. Both NASA and DARPA have had a deep impact on the civilian economy, including spurring the birth of satellite communications and the Internet. Meanwhile, President Eisenhower's decision to build an interstate highway system was intended to help American military forces mobilize in the event of war, but it also had the side effect of defining the very pattern of the nation's economic development. Like the railroads before them, the interstates defined which cities grew and which ones were bypassed.

Other programs have been aimed at health objectives such as curing cancer. The government's war on cancer led to the birth of a biotech industry, including many genomics companies and institutes. Although an ultimate solution to cancer has not emerged, spending by the National Institutes of Health is widely credited with giving the United States an advantage in medical equipment, biomechanical devices, and genetic technology, as witnessed in San Diego. "You have to give credit to the NIH for spawning that," says Gary Hufbauer, a senior fellow at the Peterson Institute for International Economics in Washington.[1]

These governmental policies were aimed at geopolitical objectives—defeating Japan, rebuilding Europe, defeating the Soviet Union—or else at public health issues where there was broad consensus that government has a legitimate role to play. For the most part, the ideas that transformed the civilian economy were spin-offs from other objectives the government was pursuing.

Other than those targeted geopolitical or health initiatives, the federal government since World War II has believed it should limit its role in the economy to regulating the private sector and to managing the ups and downs of economic cycles. There has been broad support for government to perform such functions as approving the safety of drugs and medicines, preventing crime, maintaining a transportation infrastructure, safeguarding against dangerous vehicles, and the like. There were some ebbs and flows in where government drew the regulatory line, for example, allowing partial privatization of airlines and telecommunications. But the basic pattern has not shifted in decades.

On the macroeconomic side of the equation, the government spent more in times of recession and the Federal Reserve lowered interest rates. When the economy was stronger, it spent less and the Fed raised interest rates to prevent inflation. These were instruments of macroeconomic policy used to manage business cycles, and very few Americans doubt the right and responsibility of the government and the Fed to use them.

This overall mix of government policies worked in the decades when America was on top of the world, unchallenged economically. But then American leaders, beginning with Ronald Reagan in the early 1980s, decided to embark on globalization. It was, in part, an effort to defeat Soviet Communism, but the opening of U.S. markets and borders to "three billion new capitalists," as Washington trade expert Clyde Prestowitz described it, has resulted in sweeping changes in the very structure of the U.S. economy, allowing many industries to be virtually wiped out—textiles, footwear, cameras, furniture, consumer electronics, and the like.[2]

But there the debate ground to a halt. States engage in aggressive industrial polices, but at the national level the government either didn't know how to, or could not agree on how to, improve the underlying structure of the national economy. It did not take enough steps to create the Next American Economy, to elevate all manner of economic activity, to bring about a structural change in the economy that would allow Americans to remain at the top of the world's technological and economic food chains. Essentially, the federal government has been locked in a 1950s or 1960s framework.

Now America is facing up to the enormous size of its economic challenge. It is deeply in debt and is hooked on foreign oil as well as domestic fossil fuels. It needs to create at least 10 million jobs—more if an "underemployment" rate of 16 to 17 percent is accurate. Huge numbers of Americans are not finding satisfying work or adequate health care. What's left of the middle class is under enormous assault. Income stratification has become more severe, which undermines mutual trust and confidence in the fairness of the political system. The economy faces a structural problem, much as it did in the 1930s.

So my essential question is this: If government can launch the Manhattan Project to win a war, put men in space, and seek to rebuild Iraq and Afghanistan, why is it ideologically suspect to talk about using the federal government's resources, in a consistent and focused way, to build an American economy that can endure for the next fifty or one hundred years? That should be just common sense.

Unfortunately, however, *industrial policy* is an explosive term in Washington. The very words create political gridlock, arousing accusations from its foes that the government is "picking winners and losers," which it has been doing for decades. "For ideological reasons, there is a disinclination on the Republican side to get involved with industry strategies," says Andrew Reamer, the Brookings fellow. "And Democrats have had a fear of being called socialists."

Yet the fact remains that U.S. government spending is vast and its regulatory policies are so powerful that, like it or not, Uncle Sam has an impact on American industries and does reward some companies and some sectors while punishing others. "We like to maintain this myth that the government is not involved as a player in the marketplace, but we need to own up to that fact that it is," Reamer adds. "Both parties do it, but they won't say that's what they're doing."

Some of the current calls to "get government out of the economy" come from politicians and pundits whose states gain enormously, for example, from Washington's long-term failure to shift American energy consumption patterns away from dependence on foreign oil. Because of the U.S. dependence on petroleum being shipped from halfway around the world, large defense budgets have been necessary to guarantee stability and defend oil lanes—first against Soviet Communism and now against the perceived threat of Islamic terrorism. The United States spends

$700 billion a year on defense, almost as much as the rest of the world combined.[3]

The de facto industrial policy followed by several presidents, both Democratic and Republican, has thus benefited the interests of Big Oil and Big Defense. Likewise, hundreds of billions of dollars of farm subsidies—some $290 billion in 2010, for example—have supported Big Agriculture, which is also protected against cheap imports of sugar by tariffs against other nations.[4] Those have been policy decisions that created winners and losers.

The rhetoric against industrial policy should be parsed for its real meaning. The call to "let the free market take care of the economy" often is made by those who are benefiting from the current mix of policies. Their subtext is: "Don't launch any new programs that would threaten funding for what we have." If a southern Republican were truly serious about letting the free market take care of itself, how would he or she feel about stripping away agricultural subsidies, removing tariffs on sugar, stopping manufacture of unnecessary weapon systems in key congressional districts, closing military bases that the Pentagon has wanted to decommission for years, and cutting back on tax breaks that oil companies receive for drilling? People who say they "don't believe in government" often are using politically charged rhetoric to defend the status quo, meaning the current allocation of the spoils of government. Even archconservatives such as Louisiana governor Bobby Jindal, who regularly attack "big government," called for federal help when the BP oil disaster struck in the Gulf of Mexico. If they possessed true ideological consistency, governors, representatives, and senators from those states would have said, "Let the market take care of the oil spill. We don't want big government."

Equally preposterous is the other end of the political spectrum, which holds that the federal government is the solution to all problems. Liberal commentators on the op-ed pages of the *New York Times* seem to think that government itself should create jobs, not realizing that companies should be the ones to hire rather than overloaded states and municipalities. These commentators don't seem to understand the role of the private sector and display a profound mistrust of corporations. The reality is that there are fundamental limits on what Washington can and should do, and it must work with the private sector to accomplish many of the nation's most pressing goals. President Obama was probably right to attack the "fat cats" on Wall Street, and his anger at BP is understandable, but his rhetoric runs the risk of turning into full-fledged populism that is directed against all businesses.

One fight that erupted in June 2010 demonstrated the gridlock. A group of business leaders including GE's Jeff Immelt and Microsoft's Bill Gates issued a study arguing that the federal government should more than triple spending on energy research and development to $16 billion a year.[5] It argued that a national energy board, which would include business representatives, would guide investment decisions to accelerate the development of advanced energy technologies. The Department of Energy already is doing some of this, but the proposal was a credible starting point for a discussion that should occur.

Within days, however, the editorial page writers at the *Wall Street Journal*, the keepers of the sacred free market orthodoxy, attacked the CEOs in an editorial entitled "Captains of Subsidy."[6] It is fighting language to accuse a CEO of seeking a government handout or a subsidy. That's not what Immelt and Gates were asking for—they wanted a public-private partnership that could guide some of the federal research dollars into projects that were commercially viable. Yet it was easy to smear them for supposedly seeking subsidies.

Let's move beyond this ideological gridlock to ask: What is the net impact of government spending and government regulation on the direction of the economy? What types of collaboration and interactions among governments, business, the educational sector, and other participants create real wealth and which don't? What are the industrial and technological areas in which it makes strategic sense for America to be competitive, and what are the barriers to that? How do we build the Next American Economy versus merely defending sectors that are indefensible over the long term?

The Obama administration has, in fact, been moving on many fronts in what appears to be an attempt to craft an industrial policy. These steps are different from Obama's huge macroeconomic stimulus efforts, the bailouts of the automotive and financial sectors, and plans to reform the health care and financial sectors because many are aimed at specific technologies and industries. They could have a direct bearing on America's competitiveness in the world.

Among those steps, the administration has greatly expanded funding to smart electricity grids and renewable energy technologies in places such as Austin, supported new entrants into the auto industry, fostered the emergence of A123 in lithium-ion batteries, proposed an expanded role for private companies in NASA space programs, launched a new broadband Internet policy, announced a plan to build high-speed trains between American cities, proclaimed that it will double exports, and boosted the efforts of community colleges such as Tri-C to improve workplace skills. Other parts of the federal government—the Pentagon and its DARPA unit, the National Science Foundation, and the National Institutes of Health—continue to spend heavily in ways that spill over into civilian technology. The rise of A123 was the clear intention of both the Bush and Obama administrations. There was a direct goal and direct spending to achieve it.

But even though huge sums of money are being poured into these projects, the administration does not have a coherent, integrated policy, at least not as of the fall of 2010. "This strategy is just firefighting," says Hufbauer. "The coordination between these different agencies is pretty limited because each of them has its own constituency. You would think that some sort of czar might coordinate them. But that's not contemplated at this point."

Columnist Thomas L. Friedman, writing in the *Times*, analyzed it well. "Although there are many 'innovation' initiatives ongoing in this administration, they are not well coordinated or a top priority or championed by knowledgeable leadership," he wrote. "This administration is heavily staffed by academics, lawyers and political types. There is no senior person who has run a large company or built and sold globally a new innovative product."[7] For those reasons, he said, the administration pushed taxes, social spending, and regulation, not competitiveness and new business formation.

It's not a question of whether Obama or his successor should have an industrial policy but whether any administration should do it better and focus it on advanced industries that are more important to America's future. What if Americans decided that building a real economic recovery and creating millions of high-paying jobs—while easing American dependence on imported energy—was the central challenge facing the nation? That goal would not preclude us from keeping our guard up against undeniably hostile forces in the world, but it would require an adjustment. Here are key principles that should guide such an industrial policy.

WHAT THE GOVERNMENT SHOULD DO

Expand Support for Clusters

MORE SO THAN IT DOES TODAY, the federal government should take cues from the technologies that are already showing promise in regional clusters rather than mandating technology priorities from Washington. As widely acknowledged by both supporters and opponents of industrial policy, the federal government, by itself, is rarely wise enough to pick winning technologies and can drop billions of dollars into technologies that are dead ends, such as cold fusion. The government should provide relatively small, targeted amounts of money to support clusters that are on the brink of establishing their technologies as full-fledged industries, such as Pittsburgh's advanced robotics industry and

Orlando's simulation industry, and shift funding away from those that are well established on the world stage with proven technologies. Funding should be withheld from cities and regions whose policies are fundamentally flawed.

The 2008 Brookings study argued that the federal government should establish an industry clusters program that stimulates the collaborative interactions of firms and supporting organizations in regional economies. "This nation's network of cluster initiatives remains thin and uneven," it said. As a result, many U.S. industry clusters are not as competitive as they could be. It argued that the federal government has the reach and the resources to stimulate the growth of clusters and to address the various barriers that limit cluster development. According to the study, fourteen different federal agencies spent $76.7 billion in fiscal 2006 on 250 separate programs aimed at spurring regional economic clusters, including small business assistance, workforce training, and research and development. It said these programs "have evolved in a wildly ad hoc, idiosyncratic, and uncoordinated fashion."

It seems obvious that the government should better coordinate that spending, either by combining agencies and consolidating programs or by forcing the agencies to take part in genuine interagency processes. Some progress has been made since the Brookings study appeared, but not enough. We need not incremental shifts but rather quantum breakthroughs. States and localities should do the "retail" work of catalyzing clusters, and the feds should be the "wholesalers" offering raw materials and components. The federal government, for example, should gather more information and spread best practices. It should also encourage clusters to take advantage of grants for infrastructure, R&D, and workforce development, which are sometimes hidden from easy view.

Brookings and others advocate the creation of a new agency within the government to handle this work, but we don't need any more bureaucracies. It should be done within existing agencies, combining some of them, if necessary, to focus them on the challenge. The Economic Development Administration already exists within the U.S. Department of Commerce and already manages some programs in support of clusters. Rather than creating a new bureaucracy, the existing machinery should be improved as necessary. If the current leadership is not deemed competent, bring in new leadership.

Inevitably, questions will arise. Which clusters are viable and deserve support, and which clusters are fully mature or badly flawed? At what precise point in its life cycle does a cluster need support, and exactly what forms of support? It's possible that federal policy could become skewed by political considerations to support the wrong clusters while ignoring new possibilities. That's a danger that must be carefully skirted. This task can be achieved without allocating billions of dollars more. Using the existing funding in a smarter way would have huge impact. It could all start with hammering out a common vocabulary and a common framework for assessing the strengths and weaknesses of specific regions.

Adjust R&D Spending Going to Idea Factories

THE OBAMA ADMINISTRATION is proposing to spend $147.7 billion for research and development in 2011, according to an analysis by the American Association for the Advancement of Science (AAAS).[8] That is an increase of just 0.2 percent from the previous year.

This is the money that flows to the Pentagon and DARPA, the National Institutes of Health, National Science Foundation, National Institute of Standards and Technology, and the Department of Energy, among others. They, in turn, funnel most of that money to the idea factories themselves, meaning to universities, institutes, and labs.

That's an incredibly large amount of money, and certainly enough to have dramatic impact on commercialization of technology. But how can all that spending be better coordinated and given a national strategy? Without having to involve a bitterly divided Congress, a president could summon the heads of key agencies for a group discussion focused on how they must cooperate. Each agency will fiercely protect their territory, but the silos have to be smashed. A president of the United States—acting with key scientific and business advisers—ought to be able to shape the spending to achieve certain objectives even if it requires use of executive orders as well as forceful argumentation.

The strategy should be to limit federal research dollars to component technologies. It's one thing for the government to support lithium-ion batteries, which could be used by multiple manufacturers in different industries. That gives the market a large say in how the technology evolves and how it is used. It is quite another thing to support the manufacture of a specific finished product, such as cars. The federal government should concentrate on technologies that form the building blocks of finished products, not the end products themselves, and particularly not those in a mature industry.

The Obama administration appears to have redoubled its commitment to push for "green" energy research in the wake of the BP disaster and the West Virginia mining disaster before that. But is research spending the only solution? The takeaway from Austin's smart grid project is that new institutional models, or ecosystems, can be created to provide utilities with incentives to embrace, rather than reject, newer renewable, distributed technologies. A sophisticated analysis might reveal that $10 billion of federal spending to support feed-in tariffs, which guarantee a price for providers of solar or wind energy, might be more effective than spending that same money on research. The government should be flexible enough to make that kind of judgment.

Other new models may be needed to spur the use of electric or fuel cell automobiles. Rather than federal dollars being poured into brand-new research, it may be that some of this money should be shifted to a handful of cities to demonstrate that electric cars can work, which is the proposal of Senator Lamar Alexander, a Tennessee Republican.[9] Under legislation he introduced, those cities would receive funds to build recharging stations and residents would get an increase in an existing tax credit for buying electric cars, to $10,000 from $7,500. This was pure industrial policy, yet it came from the Republican side of the aisle. And it had the powerful support of FedEx chief executive Fred Smith, whose company is headquartered in Memphis. "I'm a free-market person," Smith told the *Wall Street Journal*.[10] "I'd prefer that all of this take place with nothing but the free market. But the reality is that, to push things down the cost-price curve, the government is sometimes important." This is a major point: Only the federal government possesses the resources to take the really big risks that can possibly transform parts of the U.S. economy.

If there were ten overwhelming technological priorities, and funding were concentrated on them, the country as a whole might derive more tangible benefit from taxpayer dollars than if the funding were as widely disbursed as it has been. This would involve tough choices because some universities and institutes in certain geographies would lose a percentage of funding, and congressmen representing those districts would certainly howl. One way to avoid the politicization of this decision-making process would be the sort of nonpolitical commissions that are created to decide which military bases to shutter.

Overall federal R&D spending also should be tilted away from basic research toward the formation of businesses by 10 percent. The United States already has a cornucopia of technologies in its idea factories. The critical gap is the early-stage financing that allows companies to survive the valley of death. Ideas that might take ten years to commercialize under current circumstances could become realities within a year or two if the funding were shifted just slightly. Scientists such as MIT's Yet-Ming Chiang say it is a mistake to eliminate funding for basic research. "You still need the seed corn, and basic research creates the seed corn," he says. "Basic is what separates us from other countries." He's right that the United States should not abandon basic research, but it should increase its concentration on commercializing it.

Elsewhere, there are huge issues in how the National Institutes of Health and National Science Foundation make decisions about grants. They have systems of peer review in which other academics evaluate research proposals from scientists, whether professors or graduate students. Some experts argue that this favors older, more established scientists at the expense of younger scientists with better ideas. My point, however, is that people with exposure to the commercial world should have a voice in what gets funded. They should not control it, but their voice should be heeded. The alternative is to shift some of their funding to other parts of the federal government that have higher level of knowledge of real business needs.

There are some positive trends in the proposed 2011 R&D budget, according to the AAAS. The Obama administration would retreat from a moon-landing program, which is simply not a national priority at this time in view of other pressing challenges. The administration proposes a substantial 5.9 percent increase for non-defense-related research and development while reducing the Defense Department's R&D by 4.4 percent, by cutting low-priority weapons programs and congressional projects. That's very healthy. The NSF's funding would increase by 8 percent to $7.4 billion, while NIH's would increase 3.2 percent to $32.1 billion. In terms of raw dollars, it appears the administration is shifting slightly from spending on defense and space toward civilian technologies. That incremental shift should be greatly accelerated and the broader questions of coordination, focus, and purpose should be addressed.

Accelerate the Commercialization of Ideas from the Weapons Labs and the Department of Energy, and Shift Military Spending Slightly

THE NATIONAL WEAPONS LABORATORIES, run by the Department of Energy, are home to some of the most advanced technologies in the world because hundreds of billions of taxpayer dollars have been invested in them, over the course of decades, to maintain American military prowess. They do have processes that allow entrepreneurs to license their nonclassified ideas and attempt to commercialize them.

Serial entrepreneur Damoder Reddy, for example, licensed nanocrystal semiconductors from Lawrence Berkeley National Laboratory in Berkeley, California, which invented the first atomic bomb. Although it no longer carries out work on nuclear weapons, Lawrence Berkeley has remained at the cutting edge of many key technologies. The nanocrystal semiconductors it invented, for example, are allowing Reddy to make an ultrathin-film solar technology. The semiconductors are so small that his company, Solexant, based in San Jose, can place them in a liquid solvent that permits the chips to be printed on substrates in very high volumes. This will allow the building of very large solar energy conversion devices at very low costs. Reddy argues that this is a breakthrough technology that will enable solar farms to generate electricity at rates comparable with fossil fuels.[11] He has raised venture capital and is now building a pilot plant in Silicon Valley.

His critique of how the labs license their technology, widely shared by other entrepreneurs, is revealing:

- It can be difficult to find a technology within the national labs. The labs maintain lists of available technology on their Web sites and send out e-mails to companies in certain industries, but the process of informing business leaders about what technologies exist is imperfect.

- Negotiating licenses, or CRADAs, is cumbersome and time-consuming. Part of the problem is that the labs are not staffed well enough to accommodate many requests. They are easily overwhelmed. It took Reddy a full year to negotiate his CRADA. "The system is not set up to promote easy access by the entrepreneurs," Reddy notes. "That's a big inhibitor." He is aware of a competitor who licensed a similar technology from MIT in a matter of weeks. The labs need to become more sophisticated about and more committed to negotiating CRADAs, much as leading research universities are.

• Access to the scientists is difficult. "How the researchers cooperate with the companies is important," Reddy says. Just licensing a technology is not as good as being able to work with the inventors to fully understand and develop the technology. That interaction can be critical. "There is a major gap there," he says. "If that gap were closed, you would see a lot more commercialization."

• The labs are not as sophisticated as leading research universities in terms of the form of compensation they will accept. Whereas MIT will charge a nominal up-front fee and get most of its return from an equity participation, the labs demand their fees well before an entrepreneur can possibly know whether the idea can be commercialized. That is another disincentive.

• The ecosystems are not in place to facilitate the flow of ideas out of the labs. Universities have done a much better job in assembling venture capitalists, patent lawyers, accountants, incubation specialists, and others who are typically involved in commercializing an idea.

The net effect is that only a tiny fraction of the technologies inside the labs are entering commercialization. No one has a precise figure because it's impossible to know exactly how many technologies are suitable for the commercial marketplace. But Reddy estimates that less than 1 percent of the viable ideas in the labs are commercialized. "I'm sure there is a hidden treasure of technology if only we could tap it," he concludes.

The Department of Energy, which runs the labs, should receive much more funding to accelerate commercialization of its ideas. The department has created a twenty-employee unit called ARPA-E, modeled on the Pentagon's DARPA. It operates outside of civil service hiring rules, so it can bring in top scientists and venture capitalists. It is receiving $200 million a year, and the Obama administration has asked for $300 million in 2011. But rather than being incrementally increased, that funding should be dramatically expanded, to perhaps $1 billion. Congress also should release $1 billion in funding for the proposal by Energy Secretary Steven Chu, a Nobel Prize–winning physicist, to create eight energy innovation hubs—a series of so-called mini–Manhattan projects—that would tackle such issues as smart grids, solar electricity, and batteries. These are precisely the sort of relatively small initiatives that can make end-runs around the department's bureaucracy and have a huge impact on commercializing key technologies.

Another slight shift in emphasis in terms of how the military develops its technologies and procures equipment could be hugely beneficial as well. The Pentagon has traditionally been concerned about the industrial base of the United States. In the event of a war, or in the event of the disruption of international trade, could private industry in the continental United States provide the military with the equipment and matériel that it needs? That has depended on maintaining a base of U.S.-owned and U.S.-based suppliers. What if now the Pentagon concludes that it is increasingly important to target technologies with applications in both the military and civilian sectors? This is called dual-use technology. That might set the stage for more technologies to become "spin-on" technologies, meaning consciously crafted to create industries and jobs, rather than accidental "spin-offs." Military R&D and procurement should be tweaked by a margin of 5 or 10 percent to accomplish this, without sacrificing military effectiveness or preparedness. And the Pentagon should consider reviving efforts, such as the Socrates Project of the early 1980s, to identify key technologies in which the United States must maintain strong leadership, such as rare earth metals. The goal would be ensuring that the U.S. military can depend on American-based suppliers of those technologies in the event of a new global conflict.

Launch a High-Tech Export Offensive

PRESIDENT OBAMA WANTS TO DOUBLE U.S. exports, a noble goal indeed, but Washington does not seem to have a grip on the core of the challenge, which is building export ecosystems throughout the country that encourage small and medium-sized companies either to start exporting or to expand their exports of high-tech products. It's no wonder that within a matter of months after Obama announced his goal, a headline in the *New York Times* read, "Initiative on Exports Hits Hurdles."[12]

Among other factors, there is shocking bureaucratic inertia and infighting among the agencies that should be doing a better job to promote exports from those companies. U.S. & Foreign Commercial Service officers on the ground in embassies around the world tend to be experienced and knowledgeable, but they are easily overwhelmed by the sheer volume of demands for help that are placed upon them. The service's presence on the ground throughout the United States is thin and uneven. Collaboration with state agencies sometimes occurs, sometimes not. Funding for the Commercial Service is being enhanced in 2011, and that trend should continue for multiple years. More people with business experience should be recruited.

The Small Business Administration, which provides grants and loans to smaller companies, has been a dumping ground for political appointees for years and is woefully inadequate to the export challenge. The Export-Import Bank has issued moving press releases about the dramatic progress it is making in transforming itself from an institution that helps big companies such as Boeing and Ford Motor to one that is reaching out to the grass roots, but very little has changed. Its funding is being expanded by $2 billion in 2011, but it's not just a question of how much money its budget possesses. It's a question of its bureaucratic mind-set and psychological distance from small-company CEOs.

The effort to combine Commerce Department, SBA, and Ex-Im services into "one-stop shops" in state capitals has not worked as well as it should. That's surprising because the SBA is considered an arm of the Department of Commerce, and one would expect that they would be better coordinated. In view of continued bureaucratic impediments, the structure should be changed. The portion of SBA that deals with export finance should be incorporated into the U.S. & Foreign Commercial Service, and Ex-Im should be abolished and its functions reabsorbed into the Commercial Service as well. When it comes to export promotion, it makes the most sense for the Commercial Service to be able to offer the existing services of matchmaking and trade shows, and to combine that with working capital loans to allow small companies to gear up to fulfill export orders and to provide export insurance to help support bank letters of credit when necessary.

Even in the best case, the U.S. export system will never be exactly like the German or Japanese systems, nor should it. Those economies are organized differently. The Germans rely on industry associations and chambers of commerce to provide information and introductions to smaller companies back home, which are called the *Mittelstand*, or middle sector. The Japanese are organized much more around industry groups, or *keiretsu*, each of which has a trading company, or *soga shosha*, that maintains an extensive network of information gathering offices around the world. The renamed Ministry of Economy, Trade, and Industry, once known as MITI, and its affiliate JETRO are also very effective at vetting export and business opportunities and relaying that information back home. The U.S. has much to learn from the Japanese model, but there is a distinctly American export-promotion ecosystem, as displayed in North Carolina. It should be dramatically expanded.

In addition, technology export controls should be quickly re-evaluated and revamped. As described by Syracuse University professor J. David Richardson, these controls serve as a "disincentive" that discourages a small would-be exporter from pushing out into world markets. It is a cumbersome, time-consuming process. The Obama administration has said it is going to tackle this challenge, but it is wading into deeper waters than it has yet to understand. The process has long been tied in knots because the Pentagon, State Department, and Department of Commerce take part in it, and they have very different visions of their core missions. The Pentagon wants to prevent many technologies from being exported because of its concern that enemies will benefit, whereas Commerce is more eager to see American products sold abroad because of the jobs that creates at home.

The State Department administers the Munitions List, which covers weaponry. Commerce manages a second list of commercial items that have possible military applications. The Pentagon is involved with each. The Munitions List is more sweeping. "Every nut, bolt or screw on a weapon system may be subject to formal licensing requirements, even if similar items are commercially available," as the *Wall Street Journal* described it. "Thus, the brake pads on an Abrams tank require a license to be exported, even though they are virtually identical to the brake pads on a fire truck."[13]

This logjam must be broken up. There may be a handful of technologies—such as devices capable of triggering nuclear explosions or equipping aircraft with a stealth capability—that should be monitored and controlled, but State, Commerce, and the Pentagon block too many dual-use technologies that have possible applications in both civilian and military sectors. The era in which American technology controlled the future of the world is long gone, as other nations have become more sophisticated. The technological genie is out of the bottle. The Obama administration has issued an executive order to create an export-enforcement coordination center at U.S. Immigration and Customs Enforcement, but that's unlikely to work because of infighting among the agencies and because their information technology systems don't communicate smoothly.

Commerce secretary Gary Locke has sought to argue that new

free trade agreements with South Korea and Colombia are key to expanding exports. Some economists argue that the value of the dollar must be driven lower to make American goods cheaper internationally. But those are minor pieces of the equation. The real challenge is to attack the gaps in the U.S. export ecosystem and to streamline the U.S. government's own bureaucracy.

WHAT THE GOVERNMENT SHOULD *NOT* DO

PRESIDENT OBAMA'S INDUSTRIAL POLICY includes at least three questionable initiatives. The first, being executed by the Department of Energy, is providing a $528.7 million loan guarantee to revive a General Motors auto plant in Wilmington, Delaware, that the company was closing. The money is going to support Fisker Automotive, a company started in August 2007 by Henrik Fisker, a native of Denmark, who wants to produce a premium $40,000-plus plug-in hybrid auto in the old GM plant starting in 2012.[14] Vice President Joseph Biden, a former senator from Delaware, helped engineer the assistance to save jobs in his home state.

But this company has never assembled a commercially viable vehicle, and it's highly questionable whether it can perfect a new product and introduce it into a hypercompetitive, saturated auto market, where consumers have not displayed a willingness to spend extra for fuel efficiency. "It's a little bit like NASA and the moon shot," says Edmunds.com chief executive officer Jeremy Anwyl. "The outcomes of the investment are hard to predict. Does the vehicle and the price point and the volume all add up so that they can be viable in the marketplace?"[15] The fact that Biden was involved makes it less likely that the decision was made on purely economic grounds.

Similarly in California, the federal government has extended $465 million in federal loan guarantees to Tesla Motors, which is hoping to launch a $57,400 battery-powered vehicle called the Model S, using an old GM-Toyota plant in Fremont, California.[16]

Tesla chief executive Elon Musk made millions by founding Zip2 and PayPal, but he has no automotive experience. And as with Fisker, it is virtually impossible for a new company to emerge in an industry that is dominated by global companies with huge experience in engines and transmissions, design, manufacturing, dealer networks, and warranties. The barriers to entry are overwhelming. After its IPO, Tesla is likely to sell itself to Toyota or Daimler, both of which have invested in the company. American taxpayer dollars will have supported one of those companies. Within three to five years, neither Fisker Automotive nor Tesla Motors will exist as an independent company.

A second questionable initiative is the effort by the Federal Communications Commission to secure regulatory control over the Internet, partly with a goal of ensuring that high-speed broadband service reaches remote locations that currently do not enjoy it.[17] The FCC, under chairman Julius Genachowski, also favors "Net neutrality," a policy that would allow Google and other large users of bandwidth to push video and other large files of data across networks owned by AT&T and Verizon without paying more for those services than regular customers.

But the telecom industry argues that these policies are precisely the opposite of what they need to justify spending billions more dollars to bring America's fixed and wireless networks up to the same standards that prevail in Japan, South Korea, China, Australia, and Western Europe. U.S. companies have invested $576 billion in communications equipment and structures in the past five years, according to the firm Entropy Economics. But that still leaves America in something approaching Third World status. Most Americans have no idea that wireless calls are not dropped in other advanced countries. There are very few dead zones, where calls are not possible. The quality of our high-speed communications is not good by international standards.

In my view, AT&T and Verizon have the right to charge a premium to people who use their iPhone or BlackBerry to watch online videos or listen to Internet music. If the FCC prevails in its efforts, the telecommunication industry says it will have less incentive to improve their networks. That would mean America falls further behind in the speed of both its fixed-wire and wireless networks.

Third, the Department of Transportation has announced plans to spend at least $8 billion to develop eleven high-speed rail lines throughout the country. One problem is that some of these links apparently will be built where there is little demand for them. An Orlando-to-Tampa line in Florida will link tourist sites and airports, but there is scarce population living along the proposed route. A proposed Cleveland-to-Cincinnati route in Ohio makes even less sense.

But the biggest problem with the plan is that it will not necessarily stimulate the U.S. technology base. Japanese, Chinese, Korean, Canadian, and European competitors are lining up to win deals and may create token partnerships with U.S. companies such as GE, but transportation secretary Roy LaHood is not demanding technology transfer from foreign manufacturers or the development of U.S. enabling technologies. "The only thing that we ask of manufacturers is, come to America, find facilities to build this equipment in America and hire American workers," LaHood said on a trip to Japan to inspect that country's bullet trains.[18] But to get the full bang from the investment, the U.S. government would insist on developing magnetic levitation or other technologies to support the creation of American manufacturers of high-speed trains. That's precisely what China and South Korea have done. If high-speed trains are a national priority, then the National Science Foundation, the Department of Energy's weapons labs, and other funding should be focused on that goal. There should be a coordinated national strategy.

These three initiatives, then, run the risk of wasting money, retarding the growth of high-speed communications, and missing the opportunity to develop U.S. participation in one of the industries of the future.

. . .

In sum, the federal government should devise a consistent technology commercialization strategy, one that is supported by an enhanced export offensive and focused on where federal inputs can be most valuable and have the best cost-benefit ratio. In the key areas that are identified as priorities, the federal government should ask itself, at what point in the overall arc of innovation and commercialization is there a gap that must be addressed? This process should be conducted in an interagency manner and with some participation from business. The business voice can be heard through advisory committees or councils or other mechanisms. If government is to become more effective in commercializing technology, business must have a seat at the table.

Whether we like it or not, the federal government is involved in the economy, and must be. No nation that lacks effective, forward-looking government can compete in a global economy. Japan's politics are dominated by ineffectual prime ministers, but that doesn't much matter because a nexus of ministries and industrial leaders makes the key decisions about Japan's economy. Politicians are minor players, insulated from any real decision making about what technologies and what industries Japan will compete in. China's Politburo boasts a surprising concentration of engineers. They may be members of the Communist Party, but they have strong technical backgrounds and they have a clear quasi-capitalistic strategy.

Americans have spent decades denigrating the federal government, sending their brightest young people into other fields. They have tolerated corruption and incompetence. It will take at least a decade to dig out of that morass. Government also has not been modernized and rendered more efficient as the private sector has been. Increasingly, the federal government has taken on a civil service mentality of entitlement and is now home to more union jobs than the private sector. Those trends are unhealthy.

We must improve the *quality* of government so that its net economic and technological impact supports the direction in which the economy must evolve. Government needs to be streamlined because the number of agencies and bureaucracies has multiplied over the years and combining several of them would free up some of the capital that is needed to build the Next American Economy. The experience at the state level, ranging from Texas to Georgia, is that the consolidation of competing or overlapping agencies into new ones greatly simplifies policy making, improves the focus on the needs of clients, enhances the flow of information, and overall is positive for economic development.

Paul Light, a professor at New York University, argues that $1 trillion could be saved by a comprehensive bureaucratic reform.[19] The savings would be found in hiring freezes and pay cuts and also in streamlining antiquated systems, duplicative programs, and impossibly complex organization charts. The agencies and the congressional committees that oversee their funding would resist this effort unless a president could frame it as being essential to a national economic revival.

Ultimately perhaps the greatest power that a president has is moral and intellectual, as Teddy Roosevelt discovered in using his "bully pulpit." There does not appear to be a national consensus that manufacturing matters to the American economy, for example. Many economists argue that the United States should make a transition away from manufacturing and concentrate only on the service sector, which is madness. This is an intellectual challenge, and a president could attack it. A renewed focus on manufacturing does not have to come at the expense of the environment. In fact, the manufacturing of greener, more energy-efficient products should be at the core of the national mission. A president should argue forcefully that America is a nation built on innovation and that everyone plays a role in it. Innovation does not always involve manufacturing, but that's where the greatest number of high-quality jobs can be created.

If the anti-manufacturing perception could be softened, then it would not be as difficult to improve U.S. tax policies regarding research and development and building factories so that the policies would be more competitive with what the governments of many East Asian nations offer. It might also help overcome stiff environmental opposition to new factories.

A president thus has unique powers to define a national purpose and seek to create a shared bipartisan vision of where the country is headed. Even if an administration cannot micromanage all aspects of such an industrial policy, it should and must create a national strategy that will address the fundamental economic challenges facing the United States.

Questions for the Federal Government

- Is there a clearly defined strategy to restructure the economy so that it can compete in the world, while at the same time beginning to reduce its consumption of fossil fuels?

- What are the institutional mechanisms that need to be created to coordinate the federal government's support of clusters?

- How can R&D spending be coordinated and targeted on the mission of using existing ideas to create new industries and new jobs?

- How can a president work with business to create a public-private vision of the country's economic future?

TWELVE

★ ★ ★

CEOs
The Case for Onshoring

W HEN INTEL CHIEF EXECUTIVE Paul Otellini announced that his company would lead a group of venture capital firms in investing $3.5 billion in smaller American technology companies over the next two years, he billed it as a step to build American competitiveness. The coalition was called the Invest in America Alliance and his speech was entitled "Reinventing America's Economic Future."[1]

But there was more to Intel's strategy than pure altruism. The semiconductor giant appears to be in the vanguard of a movement by leading American CEOs in recognizing that corporate America's offshoring and outsourcing trends of recent years, and the enthusiastic pursuit of emerging markets, have given short shrift to the need to solidify the technology base that supports America's leading companies.

That's where pure self-interest enters the picture. Intel Capital, the company's venture capital arm, will be scouring the United States for investments that help the company achieve clear goals, such as maintaining the pace of upgrading its manufacturing systems every two years. These investments will, in part, be made in companies in the technology clusters that support Intel's fabrication plants in California, Oregon, New Mexico, and Arizona.

Those companies' activity "has to be very closely located to our leading-edge fabrication facilities," says Intel Capital managing director Keith Larson. "There's where all the research and development takes place. That's the real locus of people doing the innovation." If investments by Intel and the twenty-four venture capital firms build confidence in these companies, others will come along for the ride. "It builds on itself," Larson adds.[2]

Intel Capital has invested $9.5 billion around the world since it was created in the 1990s, so the $200 million it is putting up as part of the Invest in America Alliance is a relatively modest sum. The two dozen venture capital firms have pledged to join with Intel in the investments, accounting for the $3.5 billion figure, so Intel's money will enjoy a measure of leverage. One example of how Intel Capital's investments are decidedly in its interest: In 2005, it invested in Crossing Automation, a small firm in Fremont, California, that makes specialized tools for the semiconductor industry, among others. When Intel supplier Asyst Technologies got into trouble in 2009, Intel Capital guided Crossing Automation into buying Asyst, saving a hundred jobs but also safeguarding Intel's domestic supply chain.

America's largest companies have been rushing offshore for many years. It's no longer a surprise to find companies whose international sales account for 60, 70, or even 80 percent of their total sales. Sometimes American companies capture those sales by exporting from home, but larger ones tend to make their products close to where they sell them. The go-global push makes sense because the United States accounts for only 5 percent of the world's population. For many CEOs of these large companies, it's been almost an article of faith to go offshore to take advantage of more rapid economic growth in China, India, and Brazil. Often their companies receive tax incentives to locate manufacturing or research in these countries, which do not suffer from as much environmental opposition or as many class action lawsuits. Even for products intended for American consumption, some companies such as Apple, Dell, and Hewlett-Packard have long supply chains extending around the world and manufacture relatively little of their total output on U.S. soil.

MEGATRENDS THAT WILL CHALLENGE THE OLD MODEL

I BELIEVE CEOs should give greater consideration to "onshoring," meaning never moving some critical functions and some critical manufacturing offshore in the first place. Instead, they should deepen their investment in clusters that state and local regions have already created or are willing to create for them. There are two megatrends that are forcing this rebalancing in corporate strategy.

First, China is no longer the cheap labor play it once was. Its announcement that it will gradually allow the value of its currency to appreciate—although it's not clear by how much—is just the latest indication. The highly publicized strikes against Honda, which resulted in a big pay increase for Chinese workers, and the scandals surrounding suicides among young workers for Taiwan's FoxConn, also called Hon Hai Precision Industry, have resulted in major pay increases for those workers. Some analysts say the rise of this union activity is a challenge to the central government, but I see it in a different light: The government wants to move the country out of the position of being the world's cheap-labor manufacturing platform. In some respects, it may be pleased that Chinese workers are beginning to make more money, particularly from Japanese companies. That will force manufacturers to keep moving up the technology chain toward higher levels of manufacturing. If the Chinese government did not want the Honda and FoxConn situations to come to light, the world never would have discovered them. Such is the government's control over sources of information.

The broader point is that this is a historic moment for the Chinese. They want to become a full-fledged technology-based superpower and sense that this may be their time, in view of the financial and economic upheaval in the Western world. After thirty years of allowing foreigners to come into China and export their goods to the rest of the world, and after all those years of the foreigners extracting solid profits, the Chinese leadership is pushing to restructure the economy. It is undertaking a conscious strategy to squeeze the foreigners for their technology by demanding more transfer of intellectual property and by demanding that foreign companies carry out more research in China. It has begun to tilt its governmental purchasing policies away from foreign firms toward domestic Chinese ones because it wants to encourage "indigenous innovation." It has begun to use anti-monopoly laws to, for example, force Pfizer to sell a Chinese swine-vaccine business to a Chinese company. And the arrest of several executives working for mining giant Rio Tinto rounds out the picture of a government that is increasingly determined to throw its weight around. The CEOs of major companies ranging from General Electric to Siemens to Microsoft have begun to complain about the shifting business climate in China.[3]

With costs increasing in China and the operating environment there toughening, the overall difference in the cost and risks of manufacturing there versus here has decreased. A particularly compelling story in *Fortune* magazine, written by Sheridan Prasso, showed how one Chinese company, Yuncheng Gravure Cylinder, decided to locate a factory in South Carolina because it was cheaper than coastal China. Land is cheaper in South Carolina than in Shanghai and electricity is cheaper and more reliable. "The gap between manufacturing costs in the U.S. and China is shrinking," said John Ling, who runs the South Carolina's business recruitment office in Shanghai.[4]

There are cheaper alternatives to China for manufacturers— Vietnam, Indonesia, and Cambodia, for example—and some makers of commodity items such as athletic sneakers and blue jeans will continue to chase cheap labor. Long, slow supply chains for those items are not a hindrance. And it still makes sense to make things in China for the Chinese and regional markets. But for manufacturers of sophisticated products for the American market, whose products must meet quality standards or regulatory approval in the United States, the equation has fundamentally changed.

For one thing, supply chains for those high-end products from China have become too extended and too slow, particularly when middlemen, or contract manufacturers, are involved. These outsourced supply chains also can prove embarrassing because a U.S. company does not control the conditions in which workers make their products. If Apple executives were not embarrassed by the FoxConn suicides, they should have been in view of how deeply they rely on the Taiwanese company, the world's largest contract electronics manufacturer.

The second megatrend is increasing evidence that locating manufacturing offshore and in the hands of outsourcers threatens to disrupt or retard the process of innovation, as NCR discovered (see chapter eight). Where are the truly disruptive ideas coming from? Many, if not most, are still coming from the United States. To avoid missing innovation born in America, particularly for products sold here, companies need to make deep commitments to the clusters where relevant ideas are nurtured, or invent their own ecosystems of innovation and production, as NCR did in Georgia. A survey of 2,240 executives around the world by McKinsey & Company, the large consulting firm, showed that 84 percent of them say innovation is extremely or very important to their companies. Yet only 55 percent said their companies were better at innovation than their competitors. Clearly, there is a huge gap between how innovative companies *want* to be and how innovative they truly *are*.[5]

One response is to co-locate their assets and people where the action is—in American technology clusters. There they need deep partnerships to invest in smaller companies, nurture them, and mentor the CEOs so that they can "harvest" the best ideas. And they need to maintain the feedback loops among U.S. customers and their different internal constituencies involved in innovating, such as engineering, software, design, and customer service. Real knowledge is contained in these ecosystems, and it can be lost if the wrong functions are shipped offshore. NCR is creating these ecosystems in several places in the world, but now it is also making sure that it can safeguard the heart of its innovation process at home. It had to rebuild that capability. My argument is that the company never should have lost it in the first place.

This suggests that CEOs should maintain their fascination with emerging markets while at the same time recognizing that they need to be solidly grounded at home. "It would be insane to *not* be looking for growth outside the United States because 5.5 billion people in the world don't have access to contemporary health care," says Garry Neil, Johnson & Johnson's vice president. "A lot of the innovation in health care is of necessity going to have to come from there too," he adds. "But if you're not in the U.S. doing innovation, you can't expect to succeed. We're trying to do both, but clearly our anchor is in the U.S." If a pharmaceutical company is not deeply immersed in San Diego, San Francisco, or Boston, it is at risk of missing game-changing ideas, says Neil.

That may be doubly true if a new, more powerful R&D model is born, as some experts advocate. Duane Roth, CEO of CONNECT in San Diego, is one of the people promoting a vision of "distributed partnering." Roth experienced the frustration of pushing new ideas through the R&D research pipeline while at Johnson & Johnson and also the frustration of attempting to build a biotech company only to see it fail at the last moment because of a Food and Drug Administration (FDA) demand for more clinical trials. In short, he didn't make it through the valley of death and saw huge waste in having to build his own labs and hire his own staff with dozens of people, all for naught. "A very good product failed because I couldn't survive a setback," he says.

Ever since the Bayh-Dole Act of 1980, companies have had to struggle much as Roth did to build up a company. They all have to go through a fairly similar learning curve. Only a tiny percentage make it to become self-sustaining; most end up selling themselves to larger companies. "It was never about becoming a Merck—it was building something that Merck would want to own," Roth explains. Major pharmaceutical companies, meanwhile, want the ideas that young companies are producing but don't want to have to pay a premium to buy the companies with their bricks and mortar and their staffs. "They don't want the people," Roth adds. "What they want are the products. They have an insatiable appetite for that."

In short, even though the current innovation model has created wondrous ideas, it has not been terribly efficient. "We did it wrong," Roth asserts. That may be shocking to hear, but entertain a different notion: What if innovation could become less accidental? "Let's do it consciously," Roth argues.

In an article for the Ewing Marion Kauffman Foundation, Roth and coauthor Pedro Cuatrecasas argue that product definition companies (PDCs) should be created with small teams of professionals with deep experience in research, clinical trials, and marketing.[6] These PDCs would work with a portfolio of early-stage ideas. Rather than forcing a professor or graduate student to grapple with how to create a business, the scientist would allow the much more knowledgeable PDC to raise the capital and take the risks. PDCs might spend $2 million to $10 million to prove that a new drug is "relevant" to larger biotech or pharmaceutical companies. That's much less than the $50 million to $100 million it can cost to fully establish a new idea, including winning FDA approval.

The original inventors would receive up-front fees, royalties, and equity ownership, but they would not spend time on learning and relearning how to develop the ideas in a commercial entity. They would not have to build expensive infrastructures to support each idea. They would do what they do best— concentrating on new discoveries. Research would be "compartmentalized," in Roth and Cuatrecasas's terminology. "This model focuses on advancing 'products' as opposed to 'companies,'" they write. "By combining the expertise of these distinct cultures and organizations, innovative products could be advanced efficiently, making the risks and investments more proportional to—and rational for—each partner. If successful, the United States might continue, and even accelerate, its global dominance in innovative medical products."

It would only be after an idea has been developed that a major pharmaceutical company would buy it. "We don't need three hundred cancer companies like we have today," Roth told me. "We need three hundred cancer drugs for Pfizer, Johnson & Johnson, and other major companies. They have the distribution systems."

Although his comments are directed at biotech and pharmaceuticals, Roth argues that the model can be applied to information technology, environmental technologies, and other fields. "If we do this, nobody else in the world can touch us," he argues. "The biggest hole we have in our system is the valley of death. We have to plug that hole, not by wishing it away or having the government fund it." Instead, he advocates what he regards as a new, more rational model of innovation. It's too early to tell whether his vision can be achieved, but certainly the conditions in America's technology clusters are ripe for it. No CEO can afford to miss that potential.

THE INTEL PHILOSOPHY

THE WAY INTEL LOOKS at onshoring and cluster-based innovation is instructive. Larson, a former venture capitalist, manages Intel Capital's investments in companies that support Intel's manufacturing efforts, including software. More than most companies, Intel drives itself hard to anticipate where new technologies are coming from. Perhaps it was the influence of CEO Andy Grove, who wrote the book *Only the Paranoid Survive*.[7] It could also be that Intel comes face-to-face with the world's toughest competition every day.

Intel says that 75 percent of its manufacturing is located in the United States but that 80 percent of its sales are outside the country. Its every international move is watched by critics who allege that Intel is "selling out America," but Larson obviously differs. "We have to have a balance," he argues. "There are going to be some things you put in different geographies. People are innovative around the world. There are markets you want to address, and sometimes it's better to have a local presence."

It appears that Intel has resisted the impulse to shift the heart of its manufacturing process outside the United States. It has onshored. "Sometimes it's deceptive to think that the costs are always lower overseas," says Larson. "Semiconductors, relatively speaking, is not highly labor-intensive manufacturing. It's a very capital-intensive business. We're more sensitive to locating in places that have the right infrastructure support and the right financial incentives and taxes."

He thinks some CEOs are too quick to chase the cheap offshore labor. "What happens is that people often don't do a thoughtful evaluation of why it makes sense to invest overseas versus the U.S.," he says. "A lot of times there is a very quick judgment."

Intel worries about investing in so many different geographies that its activities become too disbursed. "We're very conscious that we don't want to get stretched too thin in too many sites," says Larson. "It gets very unwieldy, and any benefits you get through lower costs, you end up erasing a lot of those benefits because of the complexity."

Larson looks for investments in Intel's supply chain. Sometimes it is a new technology. Sometimes it is a valued supplier that is struggling financially. And other times it is in support of ecosystems. As Intel was introducing its Centrino chip, allowing PCs to communicate wirelessly, Intel Capital was looking for investments that would improve the overall experience of communicating from, say, a Starbucks. It realized that billing software was a problem for locations that don't offer free Internet access. So it invested in a company whose analog chip allowed better billing as well as in other companies that offered attractive things for customers to do while communicating from their PCs. "We invest in a number of areas around the PC," Larson says. "We call that ecosystem investing."

Those investments are not all in a single geographic area, but they support a broader corporate strategy. So too do Intel Capital's investments in California, Oregon, Arizona, and New Mexico. Even though Intel has 80 percent of its sales outside the United States, it has maintained a deep engagement with its home country. Some 80 percent of its research and development spending, for example, is in this country, precisely the mirror image of where its sales are. And in October 2010, Intel put more of its money where its mouth is by announcing it will invest $6 billion to $8 billion over several years to upgrade its plants in the United States and build a new research facility in the suburbs of Portland, Oregon, adding up to one thousand new jobs.[8] "When you look at the United States, one of the things we still have—and a reason to invest in the United States despite all the stuff you read—is that we have the best system in the world in terms of an efficient, transparent, and fair market," Larson argues. "That's really important. Our country risk is a lot lower. We have laws and principles that allow investors and stakeholders and management to be able to succeed."

Heeding that lesson and the changing realities of operating in China, American CEOs should start applying a new analytical framework as they consider where in the world to invest. Whatever precise model of innovation prevails in U.S. clusters, they are going to become increasingly important in a world in which the most innovative companies win and all the others lose. The best companies these days boast that 70 or 80 percent of their products have been introduced in the past three to five years. That stunning speed of innovation is what it takes to prevail.

It continues to make sense to expand in emerging markets, and it continues to make sense to manufacture in many of those markets to serve those customers. Some research and development also may be necessary in those markets, particularly to adapt products to local tastes. But a company risks losing the soul of its innovative capability if it is too dispersed and unfocused. And to serve its leading-edge U.S. customers—where competitive advantage resides—it is best to manufacture the most advanced products in a place where feedback loops among internal and external constituencies can be maintained.

General Electric has found a transformational technology in A123 Systems and may ultimately buy the company. GM and Caterpillar are harvesting ideas from Carnegie Mellon in Pittsburgh. Lockheed Martin and SAIC are doing much the same in Orlando's simulation and modeling cluster. Major pharmaceutical companies are deeply invested in San Diego's genomic future. Other major companies profiled in this book have put down bets on specific ecosystems in these clusters—Applied Materials, for example, has a stake in the success of Austin's Pecan Street Project.

For all these reasons, it's time for CEOs to reassess their global strategies. It's a matter of pure self-interest, not any softheaded palaver about social responsibility. In view of the fact that very few business trends last forever, CEOs should rebalance their strategies and rethink the impulse to offshore and outsource at the drop of a hat. When local, regional, and state clusters function well in the United States, they are very powerful.

Some CEOs of major American companies over the years have flirted with the concept of "statelessness." These American CEOs aspired to a world in which they could operate without any governmental restraint or conditions, but that goal has been revealed as being unrealistic. Leaders of German and Japanese companies certainly were under no such illusions. They realized that they needed their governments, and their national economic systems, as partners to enable them to compete in the world. They were not then, nor are they now, under the illusion that a company can set itself free from a national tether. As competition from China and India intensifies today, it's increasingly clear that companies not supported by a national ecosystem are at a distinct disadvantage against competitors who are backed by governments, university systems, and sovereign wealth funds. Despite what the theoreticians write in textbooks, the world's playing field is not even close to being level.

Questions for CEOs

- Are you satisfied with your company's rate of innovation in serving leading American customers? If not, what are the gaps in your internal innovation ecosystem and what are the gaps in your pattern of collaboration with external constituencies, including customers, smaller companies, and university researchers?

- Have you analyzed the economics of your supply chains three to five years into the future, assuming that Chinese costs and risks continue to escalate?

- Has core knowledge within your company been compromised by too much outsourcing and offshoring?

- Do you have an adequate number of people, the right kind of people, and the infrastructure in place to harvest the best ideas that emerge from America's technology clusters?

THIRTEEN

Lessons for All Americans

SOMETIMES IT IS USEFUL to view the United States through the eyes of people from other shores. Raj Rajkumar, head of Carnegie Mellon's autonomous driving efforts, for example, has been struck by something Americans take for granted—the show-and-tell session in elementary schools. Requiring that a child go home, identify an object with particular meaning, bring that object to school, and then stand up in front of the class to explain its significance builds cultural characteristics. It does not happen that way in other countries. "It forces you to think in your own terms and you have to stand in front of a class-room to discuss it. In India, that's just shut down," he explains. "In China and India, you learn something from rote and just spit it out on the exams."

He has watched how his own two sons, largely raised in America, have been shaped by the culture of learning how to express opinions and argue from the basis of facts, not just from blind obedience to authority. "The conversations I have with my sixteen-year-old, I can't imagine having with my own fa-ther," Rajkumar says. The teenager researches a particular sub-ject on the Net, which emboldens him. He then tells Rajkumar, "Dad, I know more about this than you do." And often he does.

The educational process, when it works well, encourages children to believe "you can be what you want to be," Rajkumar adds. "Parents in India tell their kids to become engineers or doctors or lawyers, to go through very established channels." They are not encouraged to pursue unconventional paths. "If you say you want to be a painter," he says, "your parents will tell you you'll never make money and you will eventually starve."

Another deep insight comes from a fellow Indian, Abhishek Sharma, twenty-nine, who left Carnegie Mellon before finishing his PhD to cofound a company called MobileFusion. His company, on the South Side of Pittsburgh, helps the U.S. military use advanced software to analyze the thousands of hours of video images it is capturing of Afghanistan to identify enemy combatants laying improvised explosive devices (IEDs). Even though he is so young, he is deeply knowledgeable about innovation. "I'm pro–American innovation," he explains. "There is a different way of thinking here. It takes a generation to inject it into the blood. That's what generates outrageous ideas."[1]

In Sharma's view, other nations define innovation more narrowly and rarely take chances on, say, a moon shot or the Internet. He argues that there are different "tiers" of innovation in the world. At the bottom of the pyramid, some scientists and companies in India, for example, are devising ways to extend new technologies to rural populations at an affordable price point. That is clearly one kind of innovation, but it is not the blockbuster world-changing sort. "We here in the United States are still at the pinnacle," he argues. "We have big ideas that require a lot of computing power and a lot of science. That's where we have the edge."

Partly as a result of this culture, the United States draws in people from around the world who are attracted to big ideas. "Here a foreigner can think to create a company," says Sharma, who does not yet possess U.S. citizenship. "Back home, the best you can do is to find a job that is renewed every year."

If one American advantage in the world is a culture of creativity and innovation, another is freedom, which we also tend to take for granted. David Steel, a Brit, who is executive vice president for strategic marketing for Samsung Electronics, the huge Korean technology company, explained this to me. Steel earned a PhD in physics from MIT and then worked at the Argonne National Laboratory before joining Samsung in Seoul. In academic and national labs in the United States, he saw fellow scientists pursue their dreams. If one line of inquiry didn't work out, they could shift to another, and yet another. "They can migrate from one specialty to another," he marvels. That type of freedom is rare in other laboratories in the world, where researchers either are told to concentrate on a specific line of inquiry or are prevented from pursuing adjacent fields.[2]

The United States has other advantages that have not been eroded by recession. Ideas can bubble up from below, whether it is a graduate student proposing an idea to his or her professor or an institute in San Diego telling the NIH what is important in the field of genomics. We have a culture that allows experimentation and failure, because if one thing doesn't work, maybe the next one will.

The United States also has strengths because of its regionalism. Most nations in the world have regions, and it is a distinctly double-edged blade because too much regionalism can create Balkan-like conflict. But in practice in the U.S. economy, regionalism is a kind of pluralism that gives us the opportunity to see what works and what doesn't. If Orlando doesn't find the right path, maybe Austin will. If a brilliant genomist cannot obtain adequate funding in Maryland, perhaps he or she can in San Diego. In the competitive tug-of-war between states and the central government, there also is creative juice and energy. Centrally controlled governments that suppress the power of all other players in their societies cannot take advantage of that.

We are a society in which ideas have real power, particularly if they can be translated into action. Americans have an advantage not only in the idea stage but also in the environment in which those ideas can be tested. Executives at Itochu International, the large Japanese trading company, for example, are attempting to develop a solar power company in California.

President Yoshihisa Suzuki says the United States has the best conditions in the world in which to create and test a business model. This is another form of innovation—creating a new business model such as an eBay or an Amazon. Yet another form is business process innovation—figuring out a new way to do an existing process better. The American ability to innovate on all these fronts goes beyond just Google and Facebook. It has long been a defining characteristic of the entire economy.

The bottom line is that there is no other economy in the world that has displayed the same ability to innovate—we created the transistor, Xerox machine, GPS satellite system, Polaroid camera, X-ray machine, color television, Internet, biotechnology, iPod, iPhone, iPad, and Google. The list goes on and on: safety razors, nuclear weapons, radar, Kleenex, lasers. We have created many industries that didn't exist before—and services too. Fred Smith created FedEx on the basis of a paper he wrote in college that only received a grade of C. But he was right, and today FedEx spans the globe.

All these examples show that we have the power to leapfrog over existing technologies. By *leapfrog*, I mean inventing new technologies and new industries that render existing models obsolete. This is also called being *disruptive*. Business school professors use that term because it means that an idea has the power to disrupt an existing business model. So all Americans should ask themselves, what are we doing in the workplace that has disruptive power and will give us comparative advantage in the world? We should not be competing in industries or sectors that are *commoditized*, meaning areas in which anyone in the world can compete. For those goods and services, it is a race to the bottom in terms of securing the cheapest labor. Those sorts of jobs are not sustainable and do not support the standard of living to which we aspire. This kind of discussion should permeate the workplace, rather than being limited to the business school classroom. The key goal should be waves of innovation that transform.

I do not believe that any country or any company, alone or in combination, is destined to overwhelm the United States economy. Very few cultures allow ideas to bubble up, and very few can tolerate failure. The Chinese Communist Party cannot do that, which I believe is a major roadblock to China's aspirations of emerging as a full-fledged technological powerhouse. The headlines pronounce that China is producing more engineers than the United States, but that is a false alarm. Their engineers are not as well trained as ours, and they function in a completely different, much less entrepreneurial environment in which the party is looking over their shoulders and controlling the allocation of capital. Yes, China has become the world's largest market for automobiles. But the Chinese are years away from being able to export vehicles to the United States that meet stringent safety and emissions requirements. When I toured Shanghai Automotive Industry Corporation's plants, part of a joint venture with General Motors, in 2008, I could see that their design and engineering capabilities were still way behind American levels, as was the quality of their workmanship.[3]

India has created a dynamic mode in outsourcing and software development, but it is limited by intractable problems in its broader society and economy. Infrastructure such as highways and bridges can't be built as fast as it can be in China because India is a democratic nation with powerful agricultural and regional interests that resist the government's ability to run a superhighway through a rice paddy, for example, which happens as a matter of routine in China. And as Rajkumar notes, the educational system is oriented toward rote memorization. India can keep emerging, to be sure, but it also faces limitations, and by no means does it present an across-the-board assault on American living standards.

Japan will remain a very powerful economy, perhaps with a twist. In the decades following World War II, its entire society was motivated by the call to "catch up and surpass the West," and millions of Japanese sacrificed long hours in the workplace.

Now that Japan has caught up, it does not seem to have the same sense of burning mission, judging from a recent trip I made there. It is enjoying its wealth and wants to protect what it has achieved. That makes it slightly more risk-averse. The fact that its population is declining contributes to a sense that Japan is content to protect its trillions of dollars of wealth in a kind of "island fortress" mentality, barricaded by a strong yen. It still possesses many patents and much technology, but it is not nearly as dynamic a society as ours, for better or for worse.

Moreover, the Japanese model and others in the region are too Confucian—only leaders and elders have ideas; the young should merely heed their wisdom. Their strategies tend to be mostly top-down. Big Korean industrial groups such as Samsung, LG, and Hyundai have definitely arrived on the world stage, taking market share from the Japanese and dominating certain industries such as televisions. But to some extent, they are hurting their Japanese competitors more than they are threatening U.S. industry.

Of course, for America to rise to this competitive challenge while also addressing its energy challenge, there is much work to be done. To begin with, the United States has to get over the era of easy money, including inflated stock market and real estate values. Americans have to earn more of their own wealth; they can't just borrow it. That means we have to stop buying things we don't need, things that only end up in closets and attics and storage facilities and landfills. It was Thorstein Veblen, a Norwegian American sociologist and economist, who in 1899 coined the term *conspicuous consumption*, a term that very much applies to the phenomenon that hit the United States during its stock market and real estate bubbles. As individual families, we must consume less energy and save more money. An economy is the result of millions of day-to-day economic decisions. America can recover if it understands the structural shifts that are necessary and doesn't wait for a silver bullet that will never arrive. This adjustment process over a period of years may involve a sense of sacrifice, but it is essential for America to triumph once again.

At the same time, confidence needs to be rebuilt. Every time I have come back from a trip to East Asia in recent years, I have experienced whiplash. Japanese, Koreans, and Chinese are confident. They are building infrastructures, educating their children, and expecting brighter futures. When I come home I see very different patterns of behavior. In the technology clusters I have examined and inside some large successful companies, people are still taking risks and are betting on bright futures. But elsewhere, too many Americans seem to be just hanging on, fighting over a pie they believe is shrinking, not wanting to take a risk on a three- or four-year investment. For them, pessimism is a disease worse than cancer. If Americans assume their pie is shrinking, the psychology shifts. Everyone tries to hold on to his or her patch and we beggar our neighbor, engaging in zero-sum behavior. Civic-mindedness and the ability to suspend short-term gratification to build wealth-creating alliances fall apart. Those alliances across institutional lines—which create economic ecosystems—are precisely what we need more of to create wealth, as this book has demonstrated.

Another key lesson of this book, as best articulated by San Diego's Eric Topol (see chapter four), is that we must take action to repair a huge gap between the skills that the Next American Economy requires and the skills that American workers actually possess. The implication is that education needs to become more of a priority even at a time of state budget cuts. Community colleges, whose role was described in chapter nine, are just one piece of a much bigger challenge also involving federal and state governments, school districts, PTAs, teachers unions, principals, charter schools, four-year universities, vocational schools, and other players. I am not sure whether Bush's No Child Left Behind is better than Obama's Race to the Top. They both seem to create distortions in testing and how states compete for federal funds. The U.S. Department of Education has been a dumping ground for political appointments, and it would benefit from sweeping reform, as would the Department of Labor, which shares some responsibilities for worker training and retraining.

At their root, attitudes toward education start at home, where children should be encouraged to achieve in the realms of science, math, and business. Motivated children supported by motivated families tend to learn. Parents also should strike up alliances with teachers and principals as part of win-win solutions rather than engaging in political confrontation that cannot work.

Education clearly costs money, and Americans have to be prepared to spend on education. Koreans, for example, spend 20 percent of their household income on educating their children, an incredible figure.

And the U.S. debate about education needs to be informed by what is happening in the corporate world. Too often, the debate about our schools is held in a complete absence of knowledge about the skills that corporations need. The reason that's important is that's where the jobs are going to be—in lithium-ion batteries, robotics, simulation, biotech and genomics, new materials, and the other industries described in this book. These fields are hiring people with technical skills and people who graduate from college and obtain an advanced degree. By pretending that a child can get by with only a high school education is to completely misread the way the U.S. economy is evolving, and must continue to evolve.

America must address the issue of failed government. Washington and many state capitals have become open sewers of corruption, self-dealing, and inefficiency. Corruption means the misallocation of public resources, as in Indonesia and Nigeria, and works against the possibility that political leaders at any level can hammer out a coherent, forward-looking economic strategy that creates wealth over the long term. We need to believe in the integrity of our leadership, and right now that is difficult. As this book has shown, effective, honest, and wise government is essential at all levels if America is to maintain its living standards and leading status in the world.

A corollary is that we need to resist polarization and the ideology of mistrust, which featured prominently in the 2010 midterm election. I like to argue that if you took all Americans and placed them on a big football field, representing the spectrum of political opinion, perhaps 90 percent of them would stand between the two 40-yard lines. Many would have one foot on one side of the 50-yard line and the other foot on the other side, reflecting, say, that someone is is a fiscal conservative but a social liberal.

But the people who make the noise in America are standing on the goal lines of extremism shouting at everyone at midfield, urging them to divide and polarize. It is more than just ideology. These are industries consisting of think tanks, political parties, fund-raising organizations, lobbyists, news personalities, and others that thrive on the culture wars. They have no incentive to seek compromise near the 50-yard line. The "shouters" on cable television networks—from Fox on one goal line to MSNBC on the other—are not interested in forging solutions to American problems. They merely want higher ratings, and the way to do that is to shout louder. They thrive on gridlock. But the ideology on both extremes is bankrupt and leads nowhere.

Instead of partisan bickering, we need to understand how to work together to create wealth at the microeconomic level. In part that requires more economic literacy. Americans spend too much precious intellectual capital on school prayer, gay marriage, abortion, treatment of the American flag, and similar divisive issues. These are not the most important issues. The central mission should be to secure the economic base for all Americans so that we can afford the luxury of these culture debates. We need an improved vocabulary and more systematic thinking about economic development and wealth creation. We should concentrate on economics in a nonideological way. As the case studies in this book demonstrate, successful ecosystems can be built in Republican San Diego just as they can be in Democratic Boston, in both red states and blue states, in both the North and the South.

Attitudes toward chief executive officers and corporations must be balanced. Companies are critical to wealth formation, and CEOs are the ones who guide companies, as we have seen at A123 Systems, RedZone Robotics, Productivity Apex, Illumina, and other companies large and small. It may be right to target the CEOs of Wall Street investment banks who engaged in self-enriching fraud or the CEOs of major oil companies who prevent the United States from adapting to a new energy model while making billions of dollars of profits each quarter. But overall, we don't want an environment that discourages new business formation, expansion of existing businesses, or the return of jobs from offshore as NCR opted to do. Much of the populism from the left side of the political spectrum is directed against all corporations and is "anti-corporate." That's not healthy. We need coalitions that build wealth and lift all boats in a rising tide. That will require the help of corporations and their CEOs. Companies are the essential vehicles that build wealth.

Immigration policies are obviously hugely important because so many of the people at the heart of creating the Next American Economy come from China, India, Iran, or Turkey, to name just a few nationalities represented in these pages. There is often a knee-jerk American response to immigrants working in technology fields because it is assumed that they are denying Americans jobs, but they are in fact creating companies and creating wealth. Foreigners who earn PhDs should be retained. Arizona has a right to be concerned about immigration because it has a drug war on its southern border with Mexico, but that should not deter Americans from understanding and embracing the contributions that highly educated, ambitious newcomers can offer. "We are a nation of immigrants," Harvard's Willy Shih argues. "We could go a long way to addressing this problem of competitiveness if we realized how many start-ups in the technology sector were started by immigrants—small companies like Intel."

Embracing these various threads of globalization—higher levels of education, clean government, greater economic literacy, strong companies, and continued controlled immigration—does not mean we abandon values that are dear to our hearts. As a tenth-generation American, I think we can maintain and enhance American ideals by becoming more competitive and less dependent on others in the world for crucial flows of oil and money.

Could new industries alone create 10 million jobs? Not likely. Even the most ardent optimists realize that mature industries such as autos, construction equipment, and aerospace must continue to be transformed to become ever more globally competitive. As painful as bankruptcy was for General Motors, the fact remains that the company dramatically transformed its relationship with the United Auto Workers and slashed its costs while revving up its design and technology clout. Other industrial giants such as Deere & Co. and Caterpillar have gone through similar transformations.

Other traditional sectors, such as aerospace, where Boeing is increasingly playing the role of a systems integrator as much as it is a manufacturer, remain critical. The U.S. information technology sector, whether Intel, Cisco, Hewlett-Packard, IBM, Microsoft, or Dell, is quite strong but is also thoroughly globalized, meaning those companies don't necessarily create huge employment gains at home. They continue to innovate—Intel and HP, for example, are making progress in creating computer systems that operate on the basis of light using optical technologies. They would allow computers to operate twenty times faster than today, unleashing a whole new base of innovation in computers and semiconductors. That revolution is not yet over.

Wave after wave of innovation is coming in nanotechnology, stem cell research, medical devices, imaging and sensors, voice recognition, wireless communications, and other technologies.

But in the end, the biggest employment gains could come from smaller and medium-sized companies in new industries. The American Academy of Sciences estimates that 85 percent of economic growth is now produced by new ideas. That's an astonishing number. And each of those new jobs has a multiplier effect, meaning that an individual making $80,000 to $100,000 a year spends money on housing, cars, and other items, which in turn supports the jobs of others.

In general, we have placed ourselves at the center of a global economy, which means that the competitive pressures are permanent. We have to invent the Next Economy, and then do it again. It is a never-ending story. I admire the Japanese for their concept of *kaizen*, or continuous improvement. One can never stand still. The Next Economy has to be dynamic and constantly evolving, and it has to be based on the continued flow of ideas and frequent rejuvenation.

The knowledge about how to do all this exists; it is not mysterious alchemy. Real wealth creation cannot be controlled, but it can be directed. In this book I have offered a blueprint toward structural economic change and a real recovery. My case studies have shown that growth—and hence sustainable job creation—occurs at the intersection between idea-generating institutions and the private sector, with government playing an enabling role. The creation of wealth ultimately depends on how people educate themselves, how they organize themselves, and how they motivate themselves. In a previous era, it was perfectly acceptable to allow Americans to pursue their interests at great distance from each other. That was the heart of the free market ideology. But in an era of tremendously intensified global competition, we need tighter linkages among peoples and their institutions. That's not socialism. It is rather a smarter, more competitive, less wasteful form of American capitalism.

This is a defining moment for America, similar to the Great Depression, when we had to summon forth a new vision of our future. I truly believe that we can recover the optimism many seem to have lost. I do not accept the conventional wisdom that the American Century is over and now it is the Pacific Century. We are excluded only if we exclude ourselves. The United States is a member of that Pacific Century in a much more dynamic way than Europe ever can be. We do not have to accept the prospect of never-ending stagnation and economic decline. In the end, brainpower wins in this world, and America has the world's greatest supply of that, if it can only be unleashed and channeled to create a real recovery.

ACKNOWLEDGMENTS

I'D LIKE TO THANK all the people profiled in this book who opened up their lives to a perfect stranger, meaning me. Time and time again, busy people agreed to take time to explain their hopes and aspirations. They chose to trust me partly because they understood the seriousness of the challenge facing the American economy.

I'd also like to thank Art Kleiner, the editor of *Strategy+ Business*, the Booz & Co. magazine, for giving me the opportunity to write several articles that became the basis for case studies in this book, specifically the Corning, Atlanta, and Cleveland chapters.

J. P. Donlon, editor in chief of *Chief Executive* magazine, helped enormously by agreeing to run excerpts from the book as they took shape. Parts of chapters one, ten, eleven, and twelve appeared in his pages in various forms.

Pete Engardio, my former colleague at *Business Week*, provided me with valuable guidance in understanding the debate in Washington even though he is writing his own book on a related subject. That was a true act of friendship and generosity.

My agent, Paul Bresnick, continued to offer wise counsel, and George Gibson, publisher and editor in chief of Bloomsbury/ Walker, took a personal interest in this book, for which I am grateful. Jacqueline Johnson was a careful, thoughtful editor.

My wife, Rita Sevell, traveled with me to several destinations, scanned newspapers and magazines for articles, and read each chapter before anyone else, offering many fine editorial insights. She was also a tower of strength in maintaining my spirits, an essential challenge facing any author laboring in relative isolation.

At this point in my life and career, I wrote this book as much for our children as for myself. I sincerely hope the wisdom I have attempted to share helps Jason, Ali and Dan, and Joshua and Arnava David, as well as so many millions of other young Americans seeking to find their place in what appears to be such an unwelcoming world.

Cortlandt Manor, New York
September 2010

NOTES

INTRODUCTION: THE CHALLENGE

1. Conor Dougherty, "Jobs Data Provide Hope," *Wall Street Journal*, Sept. 4, 2010.
2. Gerald R. Seib, "Get Ready for an Anti-Incumbent Wave," *Wall Street Journal*, Sept. 7, 2010.
3. All quotes are from telephone interview with author in Nov. 2009.
4. William J. Holstein, Pete Engardio, and Dan Cook, "Will Sake and Sour Mash Go Together?" *BusinessWeek*, July 14, 1986.
5. William J. Holstein, *The Japanese Power Game: What It Means to America* (New York: Scribner's, 1990).
6. Kevin Kelly, Joseph Weber, Janin Friend, Sandra Atchison, Gail De-George, and William J. Holstein, "Hot Spots: America's New Growth Regions Are Blossoming Despite the Slump," *Business-Week*, Oct. 19, 1982.
7. William J. Holstein, *Why GM Matters: Inside the Race to Transform an American Icon* (New York: Walker & Co., 2009).
8. David Barboza, "Chinese Leader Fields Executives' Questions," *New York Times*, Sept. 22, 2010.
9. Robert M. Miller, "Global Steel Is Coming Together," *Business-Week*, Sept. 13, 2006, http://www.businessweek.com/globalbiz/content/sep2006/gb20060913_664439.htm.
10. Willy Shih and Gary P. Pisano, "Restoring American Competitiveness," *Harvard Business Review*, July-Aug. 2009, 114–25.

ONE: MIT AND A123 SYSTEMS

1. Based on interview with Jack Turner, associate director, MIT Technology Licensing Office, Feb. 2010.

2. All quotes from interview in Feb. 2010 in Watertown, Massachusetts.

3. All quotes from interview in Feb. 2010 in Watertown.

4. Quotes from interview in Feb. 2010 in Cambridge, Massachusetts, and subsequent e-mail exchange.

5. Bob Tedeschi, "The Idea Incubator Goes to Campus," *New York Times*, June 27, 2010.

6. All quotes from interview in Feb. 2010 in Watertown.

7. William M. Bulkeley, "Obama Administration Sparks Battery Gold Rush," *Wall Street Journal*, May 26, 2009.

TWO: FROM STEEL TO ADVANCED ROBOTS

1. Michael Arndt, "Red Whittaker: A Man and His Robots," *BusinessWeek*, June 26, 2006, http://www.businessweek.com/magazine/content/06_26/b3990034.htm.

2. All quotes from interview in Jan. 2010 in Pittsburgh.

3. All quotes from interview in Jan. 2010 in Pittsburgh.

4. All quotes from interview in Jan. 2010 in Pittsburgh.

5. All quotes from telephone interview in Feb. 2010.

6. All quotes from interview in Jan. 2010 in Pittsburgh.

7. All quotes from interview in Jan. 2010 in Pittsburgh.

THREE: HOW THE MILITARY INNOVATES

1. All quotes from interviews in Nov.-Dec. 2009 in Orlando, Florida.

2. All quotes from interviews in Nov.-Dec. 2009 in Orlando.

3. All quotes from interviews in Nov.-Dec. 2009 in Orlando.

4. All quotes from interviews in Nov.-Dec. 2009 in Orlando.

5. All quotes from interviews in Nov.-Dec. 2009 in Orlando.

6. All quotes from interviews in Nov.-Dec. 2009 in Orlando.

7. Richard Florida, *The Rise of the Creative Class: And How It's Transforming Work, Leisure, Community and Everyday Life* (New York: Basic Books, 2002).

FOUR: BEST AND BRIGHTEST

1. All quotes from telephone interview in May 2010.

2. Andrew Pollack, "Pathway Genomics Is Expected to Sell Genetic Testing Kits Through Walgreens Stores," *New York Times*, May 11, 2010; Robert Lee Hotz, "Most People Carry Neanderthal Genes," *Wall Street Journal*, May 7, 2010.

3. Estimate provided by CONNECT, in telephone conversation with author.
4. Nicholas Wade, "A Decade Later, Gene Map Yields Few New Cures," *New York Times*, Jan. 13, 2010.
5. All quotes from telephone interview in May 2010.
6. All quotes from telephone interview in May 2010.
7. All quotes from telephone interview in May 2010.
8. Claire Cain Miller, "Venture Capital Was Tight for Tech Start-Ups in '09," *New York Times*, Jan. 22, 2010.

FIVE: HOW WINNING COMPANIES INNOVATE INTERNALLY

1. William J. Holstein, "Dump the Cookware, Stoke the Innovators: How Corning Has Thrived for Most of Its 150 years," *Business 2.0*, May 1, 2001.
2. William J. Holstein, "Five Gates to Innovation," *Strategy + Business*, Mar. 1, 2010, http://www.strategy-business.com/article/0002.
3. All quotes from telephone conversation in Oct. 2009.
4. All quotes from interview in Corning in Oct. 2009.
5. All quotes from telephone interview in Oct. 2009.
6. All quotes from interview in Corning in Oct. 2009.
7. Sara Silver, "Corning Profit Rises Sharply," *Wall Street Journal*, Apr. 29, 2010.

SIX: SMART ENERGY GRIDS

1. All quotes from interview in Austin in Oct. 2009.
2. All quotes from telephone interview in Oct. 2009.
3. All quotes from telephone interview in Oct. 2009.
4. All quotes from interview in Austin in Oct. 2009.
5. Lori Hawkins, "Pecan Street Project Lands $10.4 Million Grant," *Austin American-Statesman*, Nov. 25, 2009, http://pecanstreetproject.org/?p=124.
6. All quotes from interview in Austin in Oct. 2009.

SEVEN: GEARING UP THE AMERICAN EXPORT MACHINE

1. Javier C. Hernandez, "Obama Outlines Drive to Raise U.S. Exports," *New York Times*, Mar. 12, 2010.
2. William J. Holstein, "Why Johann Can Export, But Johnny Can't," *BusinessWeek*, Nov. 4, 1991.

3. Nathan Hodge, "Changes Weighed in Military Exports," *Wall Street Journal*, Aug. 30, 2010.
4. All quotes from interview in Whitsett, North Carolina, in June 2010.
5. All quotes from telephone interview in June 2010.
6. All quotes from interview in Raleigh, North Carolina, in June 2010.
7. All quotes from interview in Greenville, North Carolina, in June 2010.

EIGHT: BRING IT HOME

1. All quotes from telephone interviews in Sept. 2009 and June 2010.
2. William J. Holstein, "The Case for Backshoring," *Strategy + Business*, Jan. 25, 2010, http://www.strategy-business.com/article /00017.
3. Kris Maher and Bob Tita, "Caterpillar Joins 'Onshoring' Trend," *Wall Street Journal*, Mar. 12, 2010.
4. Ibid.
5. Bob Tita, "Whirlpool to Invest in Tennessee Plant," *Wall Street Journal*, Sept. 1, 2010.
6. "Invest in America Alliance to Fund American Technology Companies, Create Jobs for College Grads," press release, Feb. 23, 2010, http://www.intel.com/pressroom/archive/releases/2010 /20100223corp.htm.
7. Justin Lahart, "U.S. Firms Build up Record Cash Piles," *Wall Street Journal*, June 11, 2010.
8. All quotes from telephone interview in June 2010.

NINE: THE RACE FOR THE RIGHT SKILLS

1. All quotes from telephone interview in May 2010.
2. Catherine Rampell, "In a Job Market Realignment, Some Workers No Longer Fit," *New York Times*, May 13, 2010.
3. Justin LaHart, "Even in a Recovery, Some Jobs Won't Return," *Wall Street Journal*, Jan. 12, 2010.
4. William J. Holstein, "A School For Displaced Workers," *Strategy + Business*, Dec. 15, 2009, http://www.strategy-business.com/article /00012.
5. See www.youtube.com/watch?v=Dgw7I96pQzQ.
6. Jim Rutenberg, "Obama Attacks on Economy and Seeks Billions for Community Colleges," *New York Times*, July 15, 2009.

7. All quotes from telephone interviews in Oct. 2009 and May 2010.
8. All quotes from telephone interview in Oct. 2009.
9. All quotes from telephone interviews in Oct. 2009 and May 2010.
10. Stephanie Banchero, "Two-Year Colleges Seek More Graduates," *Wall Street Journal*, Apr. 24, 2010.

TEN: BUILDING ECOSYSTEMS AT THE STATE AND LOCAL LEVELS

1. Karen G. Mills, Elisabeth B. Reynolds, and Andrew Reamer, "Clusters and Competitiveness: A New Federal Role for Stimulating Regional Economies," Metropolitan Policy Program, Brookings Institution, Apr. 2008.
2. All quotes from telephone interview in May 2010.
3. Kevin Kelly, Joseph Weber, Janin Friend, Sandra Atchison, Gail DeGeorge, and William J. Holstein, "Hot Spots: America's New Growth Regions Are Blossoming Despite the Slump," *BusinessWeek*, Oct. 19, 1982.
4. Conor Dougherty, "States Move to Cut Incentives to Businesses," *Wall Street Journal*, May 10, 2010.

ELEVEN: THE FEDERAL GOVERNMENT AND INDUSTRIAL POLICY

1. All quotes from telephone interview in May 2010.
2. Clyde Prestowitz, *Three Billion New Capitalists: The Great Shift of Wealth and Power to the East* (New York: Basic Books, 2005).
3. "Defence Spending in a Time of Austerity," *Economist*, Aug. 28, 2010.
4. Mary Clare Jalonick, "Promises, Promises: Rich Farmers Get Most Cash," Associated Press, May 5, 2010.
5. John M. Broder, "A Call to Triple U.S. Spending on Energy Research," *New York Times*, June 10, 2010.
6. "Captains of Subsidy" (editorial), *Wall Street Journal*, June 16, 2010.
7. Thomas L. Friedman, "A Gift for Grads: Start-Ups," *New York Times*, June 9, 2010.
8. Earl Lane, "Obama 2011 R&D Budget Contains Bright Spots Despite Fiscal Challenges, Holdren Says at AAAS," Feb. 2, 2010, www.aaas.org//news/releases/2010/0202rd_budget.shtml.
9. Gerald F. Seib, "Time to Plug in Electric Cars," *Wall Street Journal*, June 18, 2010.
10. Ibid.
11. All quotes from telephone interview in June 2010.

12. Sewell Chan, "Initiative on Exports Hits Hurdles," *New York Times*, Aug. 2, 2010.

13. Nathan Hodge, "Changes Weighed in Military Exports," *Wall Street Journal*, Aug. 30, 2010.

14. Mike Spector and Sharon Terlep, "'Old GM' to Sell Plants as 'New GM' Preens," *Wall Street Journal*, June 28, 2010.

15. All comments from telephone interview in June 2010.

16. Claire Cain Miller, "All Revved Up, but So Far to Go," *New York Times*, July 25, 2010.

17. Edward Wyatt, "F.C.C. Outlines Plans to Control Broadband, but Not Rates or Content," *New York Times*, May 7, 2010.

18. Hiroko Tabuchi, "Japan Shops Its Bullet Train Technology, Aiming to Profit from U.S. Ambitions," *New York Times*, May 12, 2010.

19. Paul Light, *A Government Ill Executed: The Decline of the Federal Service and How to Reverse It* (Cambridge, MA: Harvard University Press, 2008).

TWELVE: CEOS

1. "Invest in America Alliance to Fund American Technology Companies, Create Jobs for College Grads," press release, Feb. 23, 2010, http://www.intel.com/pressroom/archive/releases/2010/2010 0223corp.htm.

2. All quotes from telephone interview in June 2010.

3. Jennifer Clark and Paul Glader, "GE Chief's Remarks Show Growing Irritation with China," *Wall Street Journal*, July 2, 2010.

4. Sheridan Prasso, "American Made, Chinese Owned," *Fortune*, May 7, 2010.

5. McKinsey & Company, "Innovation and Commercialization, 2010," Sept. 2010, https://www.mckinseyquarterly.com/Strategy /Innovation/Innovation_and_commercialization_2010_McKinsey _Global_Survey_results_2662.

6. Duane Roth and Pedro Cuatrecasas, "The Distributed Partnering Model for Drug Discovery and Development," Kauffman Foundation, Jan. 2010.

7. Andy Grove, *Only the Paranoid Survive* (New York: Currency Doubleday, 1996).

8. Don Clark, "Intel to Invest $6 Billion in Plants," *Wall Street Journal*, Oct. 20, 2010.

THIRTEEN: LESSONS FOR ALL AMERICANS

1. All quotes from interview in Pittsburgh, Pennsylvania, in Jan. 2010.
2. All quotes from interview in New York in May 2010.
3. William J. Holstein, *Why GM Matters: Inside the Race to Transform an American Icon* (New York: Walker & Co., 2009), 171–90.

INDEX

A NOTE ON THE AUTHOR

WILLIAM J. HOLSTEIN has been on the front lines of the U.S. economy as it has engaged with China, Japan, and other economic powerhouses for decades. As a young correspondent for United Press International, he covered the first stirrings of China's economic modernization and witnessed Japan's emergence as an economic superpower, which he chronicled in his first book, *The Japanese Power Game*, in 1990.

At home, he has crisscrossed the United States in his roles at *BusinessWeek* and *U.S. News & World Report*. He has also written extensively for the *New York Times* and *Fortune*. He has lived through globalization and studied it from numerous geographies. As a result, few commentators can compete with Holstein's in-depth knowledge of how American cities and regions create lasting wealth. *The Next American Economy* is his fourth commercially available book.